The

*Also by Christopher Douglas
with Nigel Planer*

Nicholas Craig's
I, AN ACTOR

The Word of
POD

The collected *Guardian* columns of
DAVE PODMORE

as told to
Christopher Douglas and Andrew Nickolds

with cartoons by
Nick Newman

methuen

Published by Methuen 2002

1 3 5 7 9 10 8 6 4 2

Methuen Publishing Ltd
215 Vauxhall Bridge Rd, London SW1V 1EJ

Methuen Publishing Limited Reg. No. 3543167

A CIP catalogue record for this book is available from the British Library

ISBN 0 413 77214 4

Designed by Geoff Green Book Design, CB4 5RA
Printed and bound in Great Britain by
Cox and Wyman Ltd, Reading, Berkshire

Contents

Preface

Twenty-three seasons in the game and still landing it in the right areas. Twenty-three August number-plate changes and every one marked by a new set of sponsored wheels in Dave Podmore's carport. Twenty-three Aprils of not being named as one of *Wisden*'s Five Cricketers, but that's been more than compensated for by no fewer than three coveted Benson & Hedges Panatella Smoker of the Year awards. I've got five dogs, an attractive new Y-registered wife Jacqui, and if anyone still thinks they're better than Pod they want to take a look at the figures on those big framed benefit cheques all round my lounge. A total of 18 '0's (which follow you around the room, eerily enough) ought to silence those cynics who like to knock success in this country.

And now to cap it all my collected columns from the *Guardian* are between soft covers. It's like a fairytale storybook come true. Robert Ludlum couldn't have written it, even if he hadn't unfortunately passed away – a loss which Dave Podmore was privileged to honour by supplying the black insulating tape for the England lads' shirtsleeves when they lined up in front of the pavilion at Karachi as a mark of respect to the touring cricketer's favourite author.

People say to me, 'Come on Pod, what have you got left to prove? Your last benefit produced a tidy £326,782, you're driving a distinctly eye-catching Daewoo Esperanto supplied by Ray Poole Daewoo of Hinckley ("Incredible deals from credible people!"), and your batting average is still higher than your cholesterol reading (8.1). Given all this, why would you want to waste your time writing for some up-the-bum organ of political correctitude that pays piss and has a woefully uninformative dog racing section?'

Fair comment. And it's true that when it comes to preferred reading matter I'm more of an *East Midlands Autotrader* man. But, once tasted, the cocktail of power and influence is a fairly addictive one. Let's examine my record as a crusader on behalf of the world's cricket community. 1: The campaign to prevent the Brussels mafia from changing the name of the dear old M62 to the utterly characterless E33. 2: The Dave Podmore sliding scale of match-fixing charges now widely adopted by Test cricketers from Cape Town to Karachi. 3: The equipping of umpires with semi-automatic fire-arms plus gunship back-up for games against India. And last but not least important to the pro on the circuit, Pod's Own Chilli 'n' Red Bull Sauce for drizzling on your kebab so you don't get drowsy driving to a match.

All these ground-breaking proposals were first aired in the pages of the *Guardian*; proposals which I think it's fair to say will resonate down the annals of the game long after Dave

Podmore's ashes have been scattered over his spiritual home (Wolverhampton all-weather race track).

Sure, cricket's been good to Dave Podmore but let's not be in any doubt about this, Dave Podmore's been bloody good to cricket. So as long as that's understood, I hope you enjoy the book.

Your very good health.

1

The County Arena

I have to say that the late '90s was not a red-letter era in Dave Podmore's county cricket career. For day-in day-out disappointments it came second only to opening up yet another bag of Walkers crisps and not getting a sniff of a £20 note. Every time I turned in a decent performance on the park, instead of the England recall I deserved, I got a note saying Pod's been picked to turn out for the undead in the seconds at some godforsaken hole thirty miles from a Burger King where there's no lino on the dressing-room floor.

I tell you, playing county cricket is like finding a promising-looking blue envelope among your aforementioned crisps which turns out to contain only a voucher for another bloody packet of Walkers! What earthly good is that to a professional athlete's waistline? I often meant to get in touch with one of those law firms who specialise in compensation for injuries received at work – but by the time I'd found a pen the advert with the phone number had gone and Channel 4 racing was back on again.

But the word 'moan' has no place in Pod's dictionary. I have never given it less than 110% for whoever I play for, be it Leicestershire, be it Derbyshire, be it Hampshire, be it Durham, be it Leicestershire again in '92, be it Sussex, Glamorgan, Northants, Gloucester and hopefully next year be it Surrey. I usually give it 150% for the Costcutter Cup and probably 200% in that most demanding of mistresses the Boyes Stores Challenge. George Sharp swears blind he saw me give it 1001% at Kettering in one of the Aon Risk zonals. So there's no question marks over Dave Podmore's commitment to county cricket. Unlike, say, Marcus 'sun-shines-out-of-his-arse' Trescothick: how many counties has he played for? One. Do I need to labour the point any further?

But despite the way I've been treated by the selectors and the endless brick walls of unfairness I have found myself smashing my head against, there's bound to be some champagne moments nestling in there, and here are just a few.

Michael Atherton and Alec Stewart celebrate their centenaries on the Queen Mother's birthday. Meanwhile the cheers ring out at Worksop.

When the century milestone is reached by two long-serving cricketers who are respected round the world and wherever else the game is played, there's bound to be a fair bit of media interest. From the moment the guys at the East Midlands Allied Newsgroup heard that Dave Podmore and his old mate Spamhead would both be notching up their hundredth Second XI appearances at Worksop this week, there's been no peace.

As far as he and I are concerned, it's just another match, just another drive up the A614 (or the A60 if you want to go through Mansfield). Though Pod would be lying if I said that the mere mention of Worksop didn't bring on the odd lump, as it was here that I got my highest first-class score: 37 on a surface of indifferent bounce against Worcester, with Brian Brain in his pomp and Paul Pridgeon at full bore.

As the press boys have pointed out, it's uncanny the way the Spamhead and Podmore careers have shadowed each other. We both reached the 20-nickname mark (Poddlesocks, The Spam-Man) in the same season; we're both firm believers in capital punishment, especially for people who leave dogs locked in cars outside supermarkets; we've both brought kiddies out of comas (Pod 15, Spamhead 6 at the last count, but who's counting?);

and we've both been married to girls called Nikki. The same Nikki, as it happens – I got first crack at her, it didn't work out and Spamhead was there for both of us, bless him.

But the bond between us goes a lot deeper than that – there's cars too. Since first taking delivery of our gleaming Bluebirds, courtesy of Ray Poole (Nissan) Hinckley, we've matched each other model for model, sponsor for sponsor. Spamhead's even trying to tempt me into four-wheel-drive territory, pointing out that there's room for half a dozen extra logos on those bull-bars.

I must say I was a bit disappointed in my old friend this week. Pod's not normally one to name and shame, but I have to report Spamhead turned into Petrolhead and decided not to join the Dump the Pump campaign. He just couldn't resist pulling into that Q8 at 3 am and filling up at a cost of 84.9 pence per litre, could he? But that's his rebellious streak coming out, and not for the first time he's regretted his actions the very next day. Thanks to the protest the rest of us have been enjoying our petrol ever since at a more acceptable 79.9. And if Spamhead hadn't let the side down we could have been looking at an average of 78.6.

As with all the great sporting double-acts (Athers and Stewie, Jim Davidson and John Virgo) there's bound to be a bit of edge creeping in on the odd occasion. Most observers trace ours back to a restaurant incident on the so-called 'rebel' tour of Cambodia in 1992/3 (or '17/18' as our gracious host Pol Pot insisted we call it). I called for one extra portion of pilau rice, Spamhead wasn't interested and turned his back, and as a result he very soon ran out. He was left high and dry with nothing to mop up his biryani, and I can tell you he was not best pleased about that situation. We can laugh about it now, and our understanding these days is much better – often we order dishes with no more than a quick nod to each other.

In other respects though, Dave Podmore and Spamhead are essentially chalk and cheese. Cheesey Wotsits to be more accurate, because in the snack preference department we've tended to go our separate ways over the years we've travelled the circuit together. I'm a great believer in innovation and pushing the envelope, be it Wotsits, Cheese-and-Owens or Paprika Doritos. Anything that leaves my mouth a bright orange colour with loads of 'E' numbers in other words, whereas Spamhead tends to be a straight-down-the-line pork scratchings and don't stint on the hairs man.

But one thing we've both been agreed on throughout our careers is to have no truck with the sort of practices they go in for at Fenners and The Parks. If you want an argument for taking first-class status away from the Universities, look no further than the way those students slit open a bag of crisps sideways and put them on the table for everyone to share.

I know many people in the game date the national side's decline from the precise moment when Mike Atherton assumed the captaincy and introduced this disgusting habit into the England dressing room. You'd never get Alec Stewart doing something like that – he'd as soon slit his own throat and get his shirt all messed up.

As for our own anniversary, a lot has been said and written about two guys in their mid-40s being picked ahead of a number of so-called 'prospects'. Well you can rest assured that the good ship Spamhead and me aim to keep those colts carrying the drinks for a few more years yet.

The Costcutter Cup reaches a climax as a semi-final and the final are decided on a bowl-out.

Dave Podmore is renowned for not taking his hat off to a guy unless it's justified. But no one was prepared to remove his head-gear quicker than myself after seeing Scotland's top effort on Wednesday. A result like that away from home against that class of opposition has to be one of the most sensational upsets in the whole of Costcutter Cup history.

Obviously they'd have preferred to lift the Costcutter as a result of their efforts over 55 overs on the cricket field, as opposed to a bowl-out in a shed behind the pavilion at Harrogate. But silverware is silverware (even when it's chrome-enhanced alloy) and from the sounds of post-match jubilation coming from Betty's Balti Rooms you'd have thought it was Culloden all over again.

Make no mistake, any victory over Northants is something you treasure. The Cobblers are a more than useful outfit, be it on the park or in the pool hall. I remember an occasion at Welling-borough in the Eighties when we had a fart-lighting contest as good as won. The champagne was on ice until Lamby dug deep and showed the kind of flair that the England middle order has been so sadly lacking in recent years.

So well done to the Jocks. Now, there are probably a fair few people who are reading this and saying, 'How come Pod's being such a generous so-and-so when it was Scotland who put paid to his own dreams of Costcutter Cup glory in another bowl-out a few days earlier?' Good question. Well, it wasn't easy to pick myself up but I feel privileged to have taken part in what the pundits are calling the greatest Costcutter since its inception in 1995.

Sure, you're always going to get one or two Moaning Minnies pointing out that the weather allowed only 20 overs to be bowled in the entire competition. And no doubt there are some diehards who are offended by one of the semi-finals and the final being decided by bowl-out rather than the more traditional and easy-on-the-eye toss of a coin. But to Pod's way of thinking, this is the way ahead for the game.

Anyone who was there in the shed on Wednesday can attest to the excitement of the occasion. The atmosphere was heavy with anticipation, and a fair bit of steam rising from the duffel bags and wet pullovers of the hardy Yorkshire spectators who'd sat waiting to see some play for several hours. There was also a healthy sprinkling of youngsters, who admittedly had only slipped in for a smoke, but by the end of the proceedings 20 minutes later those kids were hooked for life.

Let me explain how a bowl-out works. All 11 guys get two chances to bowl at a single stump and the team which hits the pole most often wins the match. So, if both sides get through their full stint, a game can only last a maximum of 44 deliveries, which in Pod's view is more than long enough. I've always relished the challenge of the bowl-out, not least because you're indoors and there's usually a radiator to keep your food warm on.

So accuracy is all-important in this form of the game. Unfortunately I had an off day in our semi-final. My fiancee Jacqui had just rung through with the news about the mortgage rate which scuppered any chances she and I had of getting the first Mrs Podmore out of our lives for good. That does nothing for your line and length, I can tell you. Sadly none of the other bowlers could get us out of jail and we limped out of the competition by two hits to one.

Looking at that score and the result of the final, Scotland 1, Northants 0, you don't have to be Bill Frindall to work out that only four balls out of 88 delivered actually hit the stump. Now some people might think that this represents a pretty disappointing day at the office for a professional cricketer. But as I said to the whingers in the Costcutter hospitality area afterwards, imagine what it would have been like if Devon Malcolm had turned his arm over.

Luckily Dev was to be found among the media in London's West End celebrating the publication of his autobiography *You Guys Are History*. Apparently he meant to call it *You Guys Are Geography* but it just came out wrong. Sorry, mate, cheap crack; Pod would like to wish you all the best launching your book. Though where it'll land, of course, is anybody's guess.

A hymn of praise to the AON Risk Trophy.

Some cricketers seem to be able to pull that little bit extra out of the bag for The Rapid Cricketline Trophy, others get pumped up for the Costcutter Cup and some old pros can only ever dig deep and sparkle if there's a chance of getting the nod for Sharjah. But for Dave Podmore the queen of all the overs thrashes is the AON Risk Trophy (formerly known as the Bain Hogg and before that, as every schoolboy knows, the Bain Clarkson). Just for the record, in the '80s, it was called the Bain Dawes – magic names, great memories.

The long-awaited 1997 final of 'The Risk' (as it's affectionately known) kicks off at Bristol on Monday. Though a bit of a new kid on the block, it's already won the hearts of players all round the circuit. The main reason being that each team is only allowed two capped players so most of the lads can put their well-earned feet up in front of the racing while the boys from the seconds do all the work.

Personally I find that a rather cynical view. Take it from me, when I pulled on my sweater and stepped onto the park at Kettering for our first zonal clash I nearly burst with pride. I'm still a non-capped player, having only recently arrived at the county (my ninth) on an uncontested transfer from Durham. Consequently when we took the field the younger lads not only had myself to lend a fatherly hand on such matters as sledging

11

and getting the best out of the ball, but two of the canniest old pros you'll ever meet, Messrs Spamhead and Bungalow Bollocks.

These are guys whose middle name also happens to be Experience, like Inspector Morse's. Between us we've collected two international one-day caps, eight wives and more benefits than the average asylum seeker. Spamhead was Dyno-Rod Young Cricketer of the year in 1973 for God's sake. In other words, we've played a bit. Yet Lord MacLaurin says we're not doing enough to help the youngsters. Yes, and Pod's arse is a fire engine.

The great attraction for the young pro making his way is that AON is a nice easy sponsor's name to remember for the post-match interviews – you can even paint the letters on your face with sun block if you want to show extra keenness (the 'O' fits snugly either side of your nose). And since it's an insurance outfit, you're in the box seat should any unfortunate damage be caused to the hotel room during the omniportant pre-match bonding session.

Obviously it was a tremendous disappointment to me that we were out of the competition so early on. Personally I blame the umpire. If he'd stepped in a bit earlier, the situation would never have got out of order. The pitch would not have been damaged, the bonnet of Daffy's Mazda wouldn't have needed a re-spray, none of the hospitality girls would have got hurt and we would have got away with a fine as opposed to a three-year ban from the competition.

But as I say, competitions like this are the future of the game. The more one-dayers we play, the sooner we'll see England bowlers knocking out Aussie poles and our batsmen saluting the crowd and kissing their helmet badges (although personally I'm under contract to bend down and kiss the AON logo on the boundary every time I reach a personal milestone).

And if ten or a dozen people turn up to watch on Monday – wouldn't that be the icing on the cake!

Leicestershire's Matthew Brimson (since retired) exposes himself in *Wisden*.

After a career in county cricket as long as Dave Podmore's, you've obviously got to be looking at ways to put a bit back into the game. Coaching is something I've come to fairly recently, and let me tell you it gives me just as much of a buzz to see a youngster like Matthew Brimson produce the goods as it ever gave me to smear a single or pick up a pole in a brown-trouser situation.

Some would say that at 29 Brimsony is still a bit young to be thrust into the big arena, but he's certainly shown that when the questions are asked there's one English cricketer who's ready to put his hand up – or down in this particular instance – and prove that if you're long enough, you're old enough. Turn to the Leicestershire team photo in the millennium edition of *Wisden's Almanack* and there Matthew's achievement is, for all time, for everyone to see. At the end of the day it was a fantastic effort which fully justified the faith I had in the lad.

But then I read the transcripts of conversations with an unnamed Indian bookie. It seems that the whole thing was fixed and the Leicester boys had cleaned up by buying the 'flashing' spread at 0–1! It would not be an overstatement to say Pod was disappointed. Thanks for including me in the scam, lads.

Obviously you've got to earn a living somehow with the derisory rates of pay we have to suffer (my last benefit didn't even make seven figures). And the problem is even worse on the sub-continent. Guys having to play in unacceptable temperatures, miles from a decent curry, and for what? Score two hundred in an hour and if you're lucky you might win a moped. It was natural that professional cricketers wanted something to put in those panniers.

So even if Matthew's effort isn't entirely kosher (in any sense of the word) and even though there's still a bit of work to do on his length I'm still ever so pleased for the lad. I know this is a cliché but it's as true now as when it was first spoken (by C.B. Fry, I'm told): 'If you're going to flash, flash hard.'

Hampshire's Zac Morris (since retired) receives a reprimand.

Honestly, it's getting so you can't do anything these days. According to the Hampshire newsletter (*The Southampt' Un*) my old county colleague Zac Morris has just been fined a hundred and twenty quid for having a slash on a roundabout. If it had been a roundabout at a kiddies' funfair you could just about understand the heavy-handedness of the punishment. But for a young sportsman to lose over half his petrol allowance for putting it there or thereabouts in what wasn't an area of outstanding natural beauty, well . . . two words – police state.

What with Malcolm Speed and his ICC gestapo threatening to come down like a ton of bricks on player misconduct, and Hampshire inserting a drinking clause into the lads' contracts, Dave Podmore for one is very grateful indeed that he isn't starting out in the game in the so-called 21st century.

Twenty-odd years ago, before the bladder fascists had come to power, I was involved in a similar incident on a roundabout outside Maidenhead, after one of Michael Parkinson's charity thrashes. I couldn't swear to the actual personnel involved – I was wearing Arnie Sidebottom's trousers over my head, so some of the details are a bit hazy, but several of us, Arnie included, went on to have half-tidy England careers. And as regards the roundabout itself nature took its course, and it was only a couple of years before the hands of the floral clock started going round again.

My very real fear is that if we deny promising youngsters like Zac the opportunity to express themselves, be it on the park or be it on the A303, mark my words, we will lose them to darts or rugby or any other sport where pissing in public is enshrined in the rules.

Some words of support for a fellow heavyweight.

I've got a gutful of sympathy for the lad Flintoff in his current situation. He's just the latest in a long line of victims of cricket's body fascists. In many ways Freddie and Dave Podmore are similar. I too am sick and tired of having to explain to coaches that I'm just about the right weight for my build. If I had a deep-pan pizza for every time a Phizz has told me I need to lose a few pounds I really would (need to go on a diet, that is).

Our society is obsessed, to Pod's mind ridiculously, with thinness. Everyone on the county circuit is now expected to look like Kate Moss – when I was starting out it was Twiggy – and I'm convinced this is the main reason many cricketers are suffering at the moment from stress-related problems such as Low-Score Syndrome and Getting Stuffed by Zimbabwe Disorder.

What the Flintoff-knockers don't seem to get into their carbohydrate-starved brains is that Freddie has very sensibly realised he's in for the long haul. We don't hear so much about Twiggy these days, do we? Not since she started putting on a few pounds. I found myself playing against Twigs in a charity match at Ropley a few weeks back, and to be honest you couldn't have got a cigarette paper between her and Chubby Brown, with whom she was sharing the new cherry. But did it reduce the kiddies' chances of getting their Sunshine coach? No it did not.

Dietwise, it all started to go pear-shaped (or vice-versa,

actually) in the '70s. During my very brief spell with Middlesex, Mike Brearley in his wisdom told me at a team meeting that I needed to show more dedication. He'd taken us all to a scummy wine bar in Chalk Farm where, as he assured the lads, there was some 'truly remarkable paté'.

Personally I find it hard to take a guy seriously who bats with something that looks like a birth control device on his head. And I suppose I didn't do myself any favours by scratching Brears's Test average on one of the church pews we were sat on. But even if my face had fitted into the Middlesex regime, no way could I have stuck the diet of beansprouts and bulghur-wheat salad that was on offer. I was back up to Derby before the Beaujolais Nouveau was even in the shops.

Luckily Mike Gatting didn't pay much attention to his skipper either, and if we're comparing not just waistlines but Test records, whose team beat the Aussies on their home turf in the 1986/87 series, with an average weight of 16.5 stone? If you're after someone to fill Gatt's trousers (and let's face it, we're desperate) then look no further than a trencherman like young Flintoff. From what I've seen of him the lad can do everything – sandwiches, pasties, saveloys – and he always hits the pitch very hard. In fact, like Pod in his pomp, he leaves a huge impression on any ground he walks on to.

Freddie's also copped a fair bit of stick for his limited stroke-play, that is to say his tendency either to block it or whack it at a thousand miles an hour straight down mid-off's throat. Believe me, Pod's been there. Down the years, plenty of so-called experts have voiced the opinion that Dave Podmore is a one-shot player. Okay, maybe I am, but on the day I played the shot (August 10th, 1989) it added a vital two runs to our total. It also briefly kept alive our hopes of Bain Clarkson glory and, what's more, it could well have gone for four if Jack Simmons hadn't stuck his foot out.

The defence rests – preferably on the edge of the boundary, with a little lad on hand to offer me a few of his crisps.

11 July 1998

An emotional farewell to the Benson & Hedges competition.

'Ladies and gentlemen, I think you'll all agree that today we've been lucky enough to witness the last Benson & Hedges final to be played here at Lord's or indeed anywhere else for that matter. So let me say right up from the outset that this makes it doubly an honour that Dave Podmore should be asked to be the match adjudicator [allow time for cheering and cries of 'Good old Pod'].

'If you'll just allow me to digress for a few minutes about Dave Podmore's long and happy relationship with the "Benson's", as it's affectionately known. I had the good fortune to make my maiden Gold Award presentation speech way back in 1980 at a place some of you may have heard of called Nuneaton [allow time for cheering].

'In those days an adjudicator was lucky to come home with two hundred cork-tipped and a book of matches. But of course the game's moved on since then, and now you get given that many complimentary goblets, clocks and headsquares for the ladies that you need Gatt's Spacewagon just to lug it all out the gates.

'Talking of the ladies, I'd like to draw your attention to my by no means unattractive fiancee Jacqui [hopefully wait for whistles to die down]. There she is, bending Mrs Jonathan Agnew's ear about the best way to get yourself a bit of newsreading work on Central TV. It was the Benson's that brought Jacqui and myself

21

together three years ago: Cupid in the shape of Northants v Minor Counties in the Zonal rounds. We met behind the Rexel hospitality tent for what I believe is technically known as a knee trembler. Only joking Jacqui. Actually it was the Midland Bank tent – the bank that likes to say "Yes! Yes! Yes! Oh God, Yes!"

'Seriously, though, I think we'd all agree that we've had a feast of cricketing entertainment here today. If you look up "diarrhoea" in the Oxford English Dictionary you'll find a lot of verbiage about upset stomachs. Well, I only wish those learned professors could have been here today because if they had they'd have had to add another definition to their tome. Today has seen one of the great diarrhoea finishes in Benson's history.

'So without much further ado let me nominate Dave Podmore's Man of the Match. This is an England all-rounder who's played for almost as many counties as myself. As the man himself said: "Probably I haven't taken as many wickets or scored as many runs as I'd have liked on the circuit." True, but he's certainly done himself justice when it comes to picking up petrol vouchers. A circulation problem? I don't think so. And fair play to him, he's done ever so well captaining the Leicestershire side, ever since James Whitaker heard he was coming back to Grace Road again, suffered a knee-jerk reaction and was out for the season.

'Ladies and gentlemen, let's hear it for a guy who's picked up more niggles than Stephen Hawking, the enigmatic – the *very* enigmatic – Mister Claremont "Chris" Lewis [allow time for booing].

'Finally, all that remains is to remind you that as per usual after these big Lord's occasions, our good friends Philippe and

Frances Edmonds have kindly declared open house at their lovely gaff just down the road. The invitation's extended to all and sundry, so those who want to come, just follow Pod. The rest of you, God bless, safe journey home and, if you're driving, make sure you've got a ****ing car!'

Pod's Footnote

If you ever needed proof of the fact that the Powers That Be have got rocks for heads, look no further than the decision to do away with the Benson's. Even the meanest intelligence can see that it's the Championship that needed knocking on the head. Four days standing around in the freezing cold – I should cocoa. But the tin gods have once again surpassed themselves, decreeing that no more will the Benson's reps make their welcome appearance in the county dressing rooms at the early doors stage of the season. Believe me, when a pro has to start buying his own fags again we're back in the dark ages.

2

The International Arena

It's probably fair to say that Dave Podmore hasn't always had the rub of the green when they've been handing out the nod for the England captaincy, possibly because rather than being an Egyptian or a South African or an aborigine I was actually born in England (where this game was invented by the way, Mr Dalmiya, if you're reading this).

Having said that, no one was more pleased than myself when in 1998 Alec Stewart was appointed Test captain. The semi-shaven tendency had had things all their own way for far too long. We'd all had a gutful of Cool Britannia and it was high time to herald the arrival of Smartly Turned Out Britannia.

Obviously it didn't all go according to plan and there had to be changes after the 1999 World Cup fiasco. But it just was not on to blame Stewie. That theme song was truly bad: 'All over the world', do you remember it? Thought not. Whoever imagined that would be a toe-tapping chart-topper had seriously lost the plot. I was a bit pissed off at the time, and with good reason. When you've got hit compositions under your belt like 'Leicestershire's the Name, John Player Cricket's the Game' and 'Hampy Hampy Hampy Hampy Hampyshire', you do not expect your musical suggestions to be ignored. And what, in the name of all that's proactive, was wrong with 'Three Phones on my Shirt' anyway? I don't want to be down on Nass Hussain but I don't think sacking Stewie was addressing the problem in the right way.

I'm afraid a lot of the blame has to be laid at the baronial feet of Lord MacLaurin of Tesco. From the outset I had serious doubts about the appointment of a guy whose previous brilliant achievements included the wonderful scheme to do away with Green Shield stamps. Mind you, if you'd been as close to a set of steak knives as I was you'd expect to be a bit biased. Nevertheless I believe it's down to him that England find themselves in their current position i.e. staring down both barrels of a bottomless team-song doldrum.

I understand they've now drafted in Sir Ben Elton and Andrew Lord Webber to be England Team Song Czars but it's horses and stable doors time, I'm afraid.

A warm welcome to some old friends.

Once again, our historic Test match grounds are ringing to the sound of willow on leather followed shortly after close of play by the sound of fork on bhaji. Better still, the commentary boxes are filled with the dark brown dulcet tones of Mike Procter, Gerald de Kock and Eddie Barlow. Yes, my old muckers, the Boks are back and by the sound of them they mean business.

Dave Podmore has had a lifelong love affair with the guys from the high veldt, stretching right back to my time at the Krugersdorp reserved-entry country club back in the early '80s. Happiest years of my cricket career – simple as that. Then, at the end of the '80s, things began to change until finally the situation became completely unacceptable to me politically. Still, as long as it makes Mr Mandela and his merry men happy that's all that matters, isn't it? Never mind the quality of life for honest English professional cricketers during the winter months.

But Pod's always found that personal friendships transcend government shake-ups, free elections and what have you. And I'm happy that I've managed to hang on to most of mine. There's no bullshit about a Bok and believe me, they know how to party hearty. I've had some of the best food fights of my life with these guys. It was after one spectacular session with the barbecue sauce that I began to realise what they meant by the Rainbow Nation. And they are quite superb at that game where you drop

50p bits out of your arse into a pint of Best. It's always a pleasure to play against South Africans.

And according to the latest Coopers and Lybrand ratings, South Africa have some of the most neatly-presented wives and fiancees in world cricket at the moment. The girls put just as much commitment into their toenails as their fellas apply to their fielding. Professionalism, it's the only word for it. My current fiancee Jacqui is no mug with the emery board herself, having only last year completed a course at the Loughborough Beauty and Hairdressing College (now of course East Midlands University of Hair) but I tell you, even Jacqui was bricking it down at Arundel the other week when faced with the prospect of socialising with them. The Welcome Karaoke Evening turned into another cakewalk for the Southern hemisphere.

One piece of very sad news to emerge from the Protea camp, however, is that injury has denied English crowds the magnificent spectacle of one of the most potent forces in world cricket. I refer of course to my own county's pace ace signing from the high veldt country, Nelie Voorkenbarstadt. With Nelie in full cry England wouldn't have a price.

We first got a squint of Potchefstroom's proudest son's capabilities a couple of years back when our player coach (Spamhead) got hold of a video of him strutting his stuff, and we signed him on the spot. True, the video turned out to be a bootleg Dolph Lundgren adventure but it's an ill wind as they say, as Nelie promised to be every bit as effective on a Wellingborough green-top as the Stockholm Stallion is on celluloid.

At seven foot one, Nelie's probably the tallest lad ever to turn out for us – not that he's actually done too much of that because playing on Sundays is totally against his strict religious beliefs. Which is not inconsiderably amusing when you think how much the club had to spend to get him and his wives over here.

Nelie was a bit shy in the dressing room at first – he just used to sit by his peg reading his bible and humming 'Die Stem'. But after he picked up one or two words of English, he really started to come out of his shell, and that bull-whip of his certainly livened up the post-match horseplay, I can tell you! He still wouldn't come for a curry of course because of his principled position on racial integration – which we respected, naturally.

As soon as we got Nelie on the park there was no doubt that he wasn't just sharp but genuine brown-trouser lively. He went through Surrey like a slash in the snow. True, they scored 270 before lunch but they'd also suffered incalculable psychological damage.

No question, Nelie's tragic injury in the players' dining room at the Oval that lunchtime was what made the difference between our being top of the table that first season and being unfortunately bottom which was where we ended up. I suppose you're always going to be struggling for fitness in the lumbar region if you try to pick up a scotch egg off the floor from Nelie's height, but it was a massive shock to the lads just the same.

He should be out of traction by next March, so that certain Surrey batsman who 'accidentally' nudged Nelie's plate – and he knows who he is – had better pick up a niggle before next year's fixture, unless he wants $5^1/2$ ounces of Reader's up his snuff-box, that is!

England v Zimbabwe, First Test, first day: close of play England 203-3.

You could tell by the way the wind lifted the tassels on Beefy Botham's loafers at 11 am that it was always going to be an in-and-out sort of day. The portents hadn't been good, what with the flooding on the A453 heading for Trent Bridge. Pod is nothing if not public-spirited so I rang Radio 5 Live Roadwatch to report the tailback.

Needless to say, the BBC chose not to relay my message, name-checking instead someone stuck in the same jam calling himself Hound Dog; no doubt some sad sales rep with nothing better to do than pester busy people. Pod's spirits were lifted on arrival, though, by the news that play would be limited to 15 overs and an early lunch was being taken. A three-hour lunch is an excellent idea and went down really well with the guests of Ray Poole Reinforced Doors (Heanor) Limited, who I'd been networking hard since eight o'clock.

Anyone who thinks that Test cricket is boring should have looked through the windows of Derek Randall Suites 1 and 2, where Ray and the guys were giving it 140%, and incidentally aiming the mini ciabattas with more accuracy than some of friend Nkala's wilder efforts. In fact, the Zimboks could learn a whole lot about commitment from any one of the 200 hospitality rooms in the Radcliffe Road stand. Fair enough, their minds are obviously on the trouble at home. But we all have to go through that. There was the time just after my second benefit with Derbyshire when I had to concentrate just as the Halifax interest rate was fluctuating all over the shop. But I still kept it tight on the park.

I know I'm biased but on quiet afternoons like the first day of a Test there's nowhere to touch Trent Bridge. It has a timeless quality: as one of Pod's predecessors on this page put it, the sun's always shining and the doughnuts are always £3.60 for four.

And the knowledgeable crowd is legendary. They can tell you where Parr's Tree stood, when it was cut down and how many Scrumpy Jack and Bacon Bap concessions it happily made way for.

Trent Bridge has never been afraid to move with the times. One of the most exciting innovations has been the Sky-Track digital rail-cam, with an interactive option that enables the viewer to sit at home and edit the commentary so that Beefy isn't slagging off Ramps all the time. You can even press a button and return Jeff Thomson's hair to its natural colour. No way can you stop progress.

As for Team England, they are unrecognisable from the outfit of a few years ago. A look around the car park told its own story. No more Devon Malcolm taking up three spaces with a wild stab at putting it on the spot. Instead, a neat row of sponsored cars, all the dot.com logos pointing in the same direction with Nass's Merc leading the way. A word of advice to the Zimboks' coach and its driver: Get the parking right, you get the cricket right.

England v Zimbabwe, First Test, second day: no play (rain).

Obviously, I've got nothing but sympathy for Athers being stuck on 96 for 24 hours after today's wash-out. Dave Podmore is no stranger to the nervous 90s, be it runs conceded in a bowling spell or miles per hour through a speed trap. But the way I see it, as a cricketer you only spend about 1% of your time trying to hit the ball, throw it, catch it, whatever – so there's absolutely no point getting yourself steamed up about it.

Having said that, it would be wrong of me not to accept my share of the blame for the delay in Athers getting to his ton. Like the former South African skipper, it's time to make a full and frank confession. Hansie Cronje fingered Satan for bringing about his downfall and causing him to take his eyes off Jesus. Pod blames the Thai fishcakes in the Trent Bridge media centre. They were disappearing so fast I had to jump up from my seat behind the bowler's arm, causing Athers to take his eyes off Guy Whittall. After which Iron Mike went back into his shell and has stayed there ever since.

Apart from that, I've had a great couple of days with the press boys, who, to be honest, I haven't had much time for in the past. Having learned a bit about their lifestyle – e.g. blowing up a Marigold washing-up glove to look like a cow's udder, then putting it on your head just like county cricketers do – I realise I may have been a bit narrow-minded about the media. To see one of them fill out a blank restaurant bill for 40 people is to appreciate the true craftsmanship of the wordsmith.

And the press get messed about just as much as the players by the Powers That Be. In view of the prevailing conditions yesterday, a few of us decided to spend a sporting afternoon 100 yards up the river at Nottingham races. No sooner had we piled into the cabs than an announcement comes over the PA that play would be starting at 1.40. So it's as you were and back upstairs to the media centre, only to find we've missed the free lasagne, apart from the black bits in the corner of the tin. And there's Bumble Lloyd smacking his chops when he was supposed to be out in the signing caravan shifting piles of his book.

A decision on play isn't made till well after the last race, leaving us nothing to do with the time but watch *Countdown* and compare the tunes on our mobiles. Sometimes I wonder if these ground authorities care about sport at all – if you ask me Satan's got at them too.

But as I say, I could see myself quite happily donning the laminated media pass after I retire. I have to face the fact that I've only got another half-dozen-odd playing seasons left, and won't always be driving a car with 'Dave Podmore' in big red italic letters running down the sides and a fluorescent bat on the bonnet.

And it's got to be better than working as a Trent Bridge groundsman. They had the moppers going at 8 o'clock yesterday morning, and when they got all the Scrumpy Jack up from the hospitality suite carpets it was time to start on the outfield. Still, I'll say this for the rain. It kept the place clear of all those hordes of kids in their Kwik Cricket T-shirts who rush around with bats and balls getting under everybody's feet. Bloody little hooligans – can't they go and find a couple of lamp posts?

England v West Indies, Second Test. A thrilling climax as England win by two wickets.

Apparently we won a Test match. So what? Nobody died. You'll have to forgive me if Pod doesn't join in all the celebrations and general euphorium about the Windies going belly-up and how England are poised to leapfrog above Pitcairn Island in the coveted *Wisden* world rankings.

Not everybody was at Lord's last Saturday afternoon. Some of us had a job of work to do. New betting shops don't just open themselves you know. Somebody has to drive a long distance to cut that ribbon, without always having sorted out the business of petrol expenses beforehand – it's often an act of blind faith.

Actually this is one of the celebrity-circuit duties Dave Podmore takes very much in his stride these days. Call it an ill wind, but many more opportunities opened up in the betting shop arena after Red Rum popped his clogs, and since Mr High-and-Mighty Desert Orchid decided that he was too grand to perform at anything less than the State Opening of Parliament.

I thought I was going to have a fight on my hands to get the latest gig, a state-of-the-art branch of Geo. Salmon Jnr. (Turf Accountant) Jesmond Ltd. Especially when I heard Keith Chegwin was also sniffing around. But then Cheggers dropped out, I gather because he didn't like the no-nudity clause in the contract, and it was Dave Podmore who hit the A1(M) at dawn.

Although I says it as shouldn't, it simply isn't feasible for a personality betting-shop opening to have gone any smoother. The giant scissors worked a treat, 300 notes found their way into the Podmore back pocket, and the local kiddies' hospital benefited to the tune of a £1.50 each-way bet (plus I paid the tax) at Newcastle races later that afternoon.

Word had got out that I was in the area, so naturally Channel 4 wanted Pod to do an interview during their racing coverage. I was more than happy to indulge in a little banter with Derek Thompson, put on my Geordie accent, and more important, it gave me an opportunity to parade my wares on national television. Which is what I literally intended to do – the new Dave Podmore range of National League trousers ('cool in daytime, warm at night') has a Capri-length leg with generous cargo pockets, to accommodate high-protein nutritional supplements – trail mix, kebabs etc. – for those 45-over stretches between meal breaks.

Unfortunately the viewing millions were never to know about this exciting new product. No sooner had I said how great it was to be back in the North-West than the TV bosses pulled the plug on us, and it was 'And now back to Lord's for the cricket.' Watching England take seven hours to score less than two hundred runs might be someone's idea of sporting entertainment but there's a time and a place for everything, and I'm afraid that showing uninterrupted wall-to-wall cricket is just going to put people off the game. The sooner the BBC gets the coverage back the better.

Fair play to Corky though. I've got on well enough with him in the past. I was only too pleased to be there for him during a messy marriage break-up, and Corky couldn't have been kinder to Pod during my messy speeding and tax evasion problems, my even messier shoplifting case and my very messy indeed indecent exposure allegations.

But there's no getting away from the fact that on occasion D. Cork, Esq., hasn't done the game or his fellow professionals any favours at all. Last Saturday's little attention-grabbing outburst being only the latest example. The cocky so-and-so even had the nerve to hold up three fingers to the players' balcony, signalling to Mark Ramprakash to do something useful for once and put three Bacardi Breezers on ice for when he came in. Actually, the way I heard it Ramps didn't even manage to stick one of them away successfully.

Sure, that 30-odd of Corky's at the death and seven wickets might have won the match for England. But the knock-on effects are already being felt, whereby every bits-and-pieces player on the county circuit is now expected to go out and score a million every time he puts his helmet on and slides his box in. Cheers, mate.

Five years ago I might have been envious of the guy, with his no doubt impending central bloody contract. But now with my new-found maturity I can just shrug my shoulders and laugh. All the way to the bank, actually, thanks to a little bird not unadjacent to Geo. Salmon Jnr. (Turf Accountant), Jesmond Ltd who advised me to put my entire appearance fee on the remote possibility of South Africa somehow contriving to unexpectedly lose their bid for the 2006 World Cup.

Sorry Corky – didn't get that result, did you? Good luck in the rest of the series!

Australia v Pakistan ODI marred by missile-throwing incident.

Dave Podmore has a set of simple rules by which he lives his life and conducts his daily business. They're the sort of thing most professional sportsmen in the 21st century would have no problem with. Like when you're having a meal out, don't order anything that's chalked up on a blackboard, as the chances are it's never been near a microwave . . . When you call the lady in your life from Cinderella Rockefellas or wherever to say you're unavoidably detained in a post-match team talk, always make sure you switch the mobile off afterwards . . . Always check that any video you rent from Blockbuster for the team bus has a label on it saying 'Contains nudity and sexual swearing' . . . When you're at a filling station, always remember you're an ambassador for cricket, so never open a packet of crisps until you're out of the shop. Pretty obvious stuff but it gets Pod by.

Now here's one to add to the list: when you're at Lord's at the end of a one-day game, never ever lob a can of beer to a pal as a friendly gesture. It just isn't worth all the bother you'll get. You'd think I'd done something criminal, the way the papers were going on about it at the weekend. There was even a guy at the *Telegraph* (whose sound views I normally have a lot of time for) recommending attaching electrodes to the perpetrator's privates.

Fortunately for your correspondent, Sky's exciting new digital Hooli-cam made a right horlicks of it, and instead of singling me out it zoomed in on some Pakistani lad who had nothing to do with it. Mind you, there was obviously something he'd been guilty of during the game already, like wearing a green T-shirt, so British justice was the winner on the day.

Still, it just goes to show that you can't always trust this new technology. Even the supposedly infallible Hawk-Eye system, which followed the beer can's trajectory through the air, showed it landing smack on Ricky Ponting's nose, not Michael Bevan's. Pod's got a funny feeling Dickie Bird wouldn't have made a mistake like that.

But let's not blow things up out of all perspective and obscure the real reason for taking the action I did. Obviously there were a fair few bottles of champagne etc. being handed round the Aussie dressing room after their magnificent effort, in the face of Pakistan's unexpected and downright underhand tactics – there were times in the match when it looked like they were actually trying to win.

Anyway, the last thing you want on a celebration balcony when you've got a thirst on is to have to waste your hard-earned refreshment by spraying it over a load of sad punters gathered down below. Module 6-level students at the Dave Podmore Academy of Cricketing Excellence are currently studying the fine art of achieving maximum wetness with minimum loss of liquid. We've got a little lass from Beeston – I was watching her strut her stuff with a can of Tennent's the other day and I tell you, I could have been looking at a young Merv Hughes. You just get a feeling about these things.

My comradely tossing of an extra tinny to Michael Bevan has its roots in the time we were both on Yorkshire's books. He was their overseas player and I was coaching the nippers – briefly, alas, as Dave Podmore and the committee didn't see eye to eye over their short-sighted policy of encouraging young kids from Bradford to become spinners. Who was proved right is all I'll say about that.

So there was a parting of the waves, though not before Bev and I had bonded. What united us was not just a shared dislike of the short ball but our never-say-die determination to take on the Harry Ramsden's Challenge: neck an entire haddock and get one free. I even managed to pull a few showbiz strings with the TV bosses in Leeds and got Bev into the coveted Dictionary Corner spot on *Countdown*.

Regular readers will know that Pod and Carol Vorderman go back a long way, and in fact Jacqui and I were recent guests of Vorders on her pilot makeover show, *Carol Vorderman's Better Fiancees*. But sadly, Michael Bevan never got the nod for *Countdown* again after he slagged off the Oxford English Dictionary for not including 'cripes' and 'strewth'.

And now, apparently, the gloves are off and the truce with the Aussies is over. What with Steve Waugh banging on again about the crowd and how somebody's going to get killed, and Brett Lee thinking he's going to go blind any minute, we might just have found their achilles heel.

Let's face it, if they're going to run and hide in the pavilion every time someone coughs in the crowd, it's going to slow things down to the point where an Ashes Test might well go into the third or even a fourth day. So the ECB's refusal to give in to the skipper's safety demands could be a very smart marketing move on their part. After all, there's radio hats to sell.

An emotional farewell to the season.

It's no secret that Chris Lewis and Dave Podmore haven't always seen eye to eye in the past. I've had occasion to question his enigmatic attitude ever since the '93–94 tour of the West Indies. I'm still waiting for his share of the mini-moke hire from Trinidad.

So Chris may be a bit short of pace when it comes to putting his hand in his pocket, but I reckon he was laser sharp when he described the England selectors as 'A Bag of Shit'. I wish I could come up with a few quick-fire one-liners like that (I've been struggling a bit lately with my after-dinner speeches). And you'd have to say he's got it about right.

Being left out of the provisional 37-strong squad for next year's World Cup must have come as a massive blow to Chris's ego, as it did to mine, not to mention Pete Hartley, who apparently chucked his mobile down the dressing-room toilet when he heard the news. These blazer-wearing, gin-swilling dodderers like Gooch and Gatting have no idea the effect they have on us pros. They're messing with guys' careers, it's as simple as that.

In fact I'd go further than Chris Lewis in cataloguing the current malaise. The whole country's a bag of shit if you ask me.

You would have thought, wouldn't you, that producing a computer cricket game called *English County Captain* (Compupodsports, £39.99) – complete with realistic match situations and expert commentary by Ralph Dellor – might have attracted some financial support from the ECB. After all, they've ploughed enough cash into their 'Cricket – It's Wicked' video (available free to all inner-city kids – stolen VCR not included).

But no. Knock knock, who's there? Mr Ahmed from HM Customs and Excise. 'It has come to our notice, Mr Podmore, blah blah blah . . .' To cut a long story short, it seems that a few busy-body punters with no sense of humour have taken exception to some of the contents of the software package. But as I tried to explain, 'fun for ALL the family' means exactly that. Something for everybody – dads included. Hence the lunch and tea-time entertainment sections.

After all, no one in their right mind is going to watch 17 megabytes of unrelieved county cricket, are they? If that's what you want, you can get in the car and drive to Worcester or Chelmsford – and get wet for your trouble. Pod'll gladly send you a road map. No, what you want from the virtual summer game is razzmatazz and a bit of sauciness. (I'd also like to point out that during the recording of the special footage, no animal was harmed.)

Nevertheless, Lord MacLaurin and the Powers That Be have not only refused to stock *English County Captain* in the Lord's shop (and Tesco's) but have distanced the ECB from having anything to do with it. Thank you very much for your forward thinking, my noble Lord.

So it's with a not inconsiderable sigh of relief that Pod will be leaving these shores (and this column) at 4 am tomorrow. Australia is a country I've got a lot of time for. They have a strange habit Down Under: they don't knock success, and, stranger still, they give you the opportunity to make the best use of your talents. You could call it the Land of the Nod.

45

3

The Media Arena

I often think that being a county cricketer is very like being a great actor or an opera singer such as Pavarotti or Charlotte Church. You have an audience, you have a stage (the park), you get slagged off by the media and you go for a curry afterwards. It's virtually the same job.

I have always regarded myself as a showman as much as a bits-and-pieces specialist who can bung up an end and give it some tap in a run drought. What the public want, be they at Covent Garden or be they at Coventry's lovely Rentokil ground, is not just a smartly-turned-out professional (although neatness is important). They are looking to be entertained. Some of my tricks, like pretending to be blind, walking onto the pitch with an umbrella, taking off a coloured chap and running in to bowl without the ball in my hand are among the best-loved features of an English summer. Obviously, it's nice to be known as the Clown Prince of Cricket but, the way I see it, I am really only doing my job.

Dave Podmore has never been in the business of hiding his light under a bush – although I did sneak behind a rubber plant for a smoke once at Mike Brearley's house. But the point is I have never ruled myself out of any aspect of the cultural life of our great nation (the UK), albeit on the park, the pro-celebrity fishing circuit, the Q&A Roadshow circuit, the fund-raising and consultancy circuit or the rarefied circuit of art and literature.

Quite simply, if you are in the glare of the public spotlight then you have to relish the cauldron of the media fast lane.

An emergency call-up to the England tour party.

At the start of the week I was doing what most professional cricketers do at this time of year: sitting in my armchair gearing myself up to do a pantomime matinee. Not many people realise the demands that panto makes on an athlete's physique. For ten shows a week you're throwing bags of sweets to kiddies 30 or 40 yards away, further for those in the upper circle.

It's all about fitness. Your commitment has to be 350% minimum. It's one thing trying to read Shane Warne when it's turning square at Sydney, but you try facing up to June Whitfield when she's on song at the Reading Hexagon. It's a different ball game – although they both wear a lot of make-up obviously.

So literally the last thing Dave Podmore was expecting was a phone call asking him to go and join the England lads in the Caribbean. Since the outset of Bumble Lloydy's enlightened regime it's been the practice to draft in a number of seasoned senior pros ready and willing to impart the fruits of their experience.

Especially after the wheels came off last winter, when the Zimbabwean Powers That Be failed to realise that touring cricketers have better things to do in their busy schedule than traipse round game reserves and shake hands with every Tom, Dick and Olu. So what was clearly required was some kind of

Diplomacy Supremo, or PR Czar if you prefer, to keep matters on a friendly footing.

Sadly Geoff Boycott, who naturally was top of the list, found himself unexpectedly having to deal with what the French police refer to as Une Domestique. It's not Pod's place to comment on the rights and wrongs of the situation, but let's suffice it to say that Boycs assured me himself that it was a total accident. He and his lady friend were dancing the night away on the Riviera apparently, and she took her eye for a fatal second off Geoff's

Gucci wristbag during a frenetic bit of the Bossa Nova. Result? Two shiners.

Besides, anyone who's played with him will tell you that a strike rate of 20 in five minutes is just not Sir Geoffrey's style. Any road up, D.V. Podmore finds himself looking for a plane ticket to calypso-land, while the Lewisham Civic Hall finds itself looking for a replacement Baron Hardup.

I'm no stranger to the Caribbean, ever since the Under-14 Schoolboys tour when I was lucky enough to room with a tousle-haired young shaver called D.I. Gower Esq. 'Lubo' was very much the star of the side, and even then knew how to track down a bottle of something cold and acceptable.

Consequently our results were patchy. Runs in the sun were hard to come by, and we were skittled out for less than 50 in one match by the young Curtly Ambrose. Curtly was only 18 months old at the time, but he was still too quick for most of us. Backed up by a poor pitch and biased umpiring, we never really had a price against him. We used to pray for the drinks break when his mum would take him off for a feed.

So, as I say, Pod's got a lot to offer in the words-to-the-wise department. Take the omniportant question of what reading matter to take on tour. Some people think that Goughie has had to pull out of the squad because he's carrying an injury. Correction: what he's actually been carrying is Nelson Mandela's auto-biography. He's been trying to finish it since the South African tour and it's eventually done his back in.

What he should've done – and if only they'd got in touch with me sooner – was tuck an issue of my personal favourite, *The Puzzler*, in his kitbag. It'll see you through five Tests and one-dayers plus there's a stunna on the front cover to take your mind off all the hospitality girls you've left behind.

Facing up to the challenge of cricket's new technology.

Obviously, getting the nod to become a Channel 4 commentator would be the icing on the cake for Dave Podmore. I've set out my stall to give myself the best credentials for the job: nose stud, pierced nipples etc. etc. But no contract as yet, so it's a bit like having the icing and the cherry with the cake still unconfirmed.

I'm not saying they're pissing me around or anything. I've had a very enjoyable couple of weeks helping the Channel 4 guys road-test the new technology. I don't want to give too much away, but here are some of the gizmos and innovations you'll be seeing on your screens this summer.

The Snickometer is already such a well-loved feature of the cricketing landscape, readers will be pleased to hear of several other measuring devices. The Bungometer, for example, was put through its paces at Northampton during the Pakistan v Bangladesh World Cup match and came through with flying colours. Top marks too for the Freebiometer, which monitors the time it takes to get corporate fat-cats back from their hospitality lunches.

At the time of writing there's still some fine-tuning needed on the pre-match-interview Hopefullyometer. It monitored Nass Hussain's strike-rate at only 7.3 'hopefullys' per minute, whereas anyone who's ever had a conversation with the skipper knows it's up there in the every-other-word bracket.

And was Pod's face red after the trials of the new Ump-cam in Peter Willey's hat. I forgot to switch it off when I put it in the back seat of my car after the day's work at Edgbaston. Which meant that it recorded with rather too much accuracy every minute of my evening's extra-murals with a certain public relations officer. Still, at least it proved Dave Podmore isn't gay.

Now some people might think that would count against me with Channel 4, and explain why I haven't had the nod, or even a saucy wink come to that. But actually I hear that they're editing the footage at this moment, with a view to showing it in the middle of the night.

As it happens, I'm no stranger to the post-watershed time-slot, as any insomniac in the Central TV area with an interest in fishing may remember. 'With Pod and Line' was a high-quality pilot with massive ratings potential. And if the TV bosses had only put it out at the proper hour it would have swept the board at the Baftas and there wouldn't be a tench left in the Trent.

So, all in all, Dave Podmore's credentials are pretty well unimpeachable. And come Thursday I'm confident there'll be a space in the Lord's car park. I bloody hope so – I can't face another week sleeping at Scratchwood Services.

A memoir of the World Cup.

To be honest, there's only one word to describe Dave Podmore's mood this time last month – very disappointed. The new Media Centre at Lord's – popularly known as the 'Pod' – was surely crying out to be officially opened by its namesake, and I might add that I'd bunged a couple of bright boys at Radio Leicester six hundred quid in cash to come up with a bloody cracking twenty-minute speech with which to grace said ceremony.

But there wasn't so much as an invitation, not even after I'd offered to throw in a six-hour tape of ambient crowd noise, to make the media guys feel a bit less cut off from the outside world. It was all specially recorded, and the effects included 'streaker reaction', 'good-natured racist chants' and 'appreciation of attractive young lady carrying tray of drinks'.

By all accounts the design of the Media Centre has been bungled anyway – how on earth a hard-working journalist is supposed to get his trolley full of sponsors' complimentary booze and merchandise down all those steps, God only knows.

Disappointment number two has to be not getting the nod to make the final cut for the last fifteen for the World Cup squad. Being rejected by England was a bitter enough pill to take, but I had high hopes of opening the batting (or the bowling) for Scotland, especially in view of my widely-publicised partiality to Glasgow's national dish, the deep-fried Mars Bar.

Granted I'd have been among the older players taking the

field in the tournament. But any neutral observer will tell you that in the waistband department there's a lot less of me than Shane Warne, I'm distinctly sharper around the park than Arjuna Ranatunga and, on my day, a good two yards faster than Bully Austin. That guy gets the ball down the other end about as quickly as Bob Willis says 'Shivnarine Chanderpaul'. Yet despite these unimpeachable credentials it was 'thanks, but noo thanks' from the Auld Country.

And I won't begin to go into the rudeness with which Kenya rejected the offer of my services. Their match against South Africa in Amsterdam would have been the perfect stage for Pod to display his one-day skills. If you get a ferry early enough you can be over the Belgian border by 8 am, and loading up the team coach with beer by 9. With an allowance of 90-odd litres per Kenyan this would have been a massive total – and one surely ungettable by the South Africans, what with their clean-living religious beliefs. So once again it was a no-cigar situation for Pod, much less a drum of 500 panatellas for a couple of quid.

I'm relieved to say that I wasn't cut out of the World Cup completely. I couldn't not be flattered to be invited to help the Pakistani lads resolve some of their internecine difficulties in the days leading up to the final. As an expert on pre-match bonding, practical jokes, etc. I was the logical consultant. But it may have been an error of judgment to introduce them to quite so many casinos in the West Midlands, many of them also offering inti-mate dancing of a non-religious nature and refreshments of a not necessarily non-alcoholic variety.

The next thing you know the papers are full of it and Pod's effigy is being carried around on a donkey in Karachi. But why

I'm really kicking myself is that I didn't do myself justice on the day. I should have listened to the words of advice being whispered in my shell-like and stuck my house on the result of the final. Then they could have stoned it as much as they liked.

A fitting memorial to the Queen of Hearts.

If you look it up in *Wisden*'s you'll see that Pod's chest measurement is normally around the 42–44 mark. But after this week's call from Lord's I can report that it's swelled right up into the low 50s. Getting the nod to be on the advisory committee for the most important game of the season is the highest accolade an ordinary cricketer (albeit one who never gives much away outside the off peg) could wish for.

The MCC v Rest of the World match on 18 July is the jewel in the crown of this summer's tributes to Diana, Princess of Wales. Little did I think when I checked my messages after coming back from a morning's bulk-buying at Dog Food World that I was about to become a pearl or at the very least a couple of carats in that jewel.

With eight benefits already under my belt, Pod's fund-raising activities are widely agreed to be world-class. But it was still a bit of a shock to be drafted onto the MCC committee after my record at headquarters. I once foolishly walked into the pavilion wearing a jacket that wasn't covered in dandruff and fag-burns, and Gubby Allen never did see the funny side of the half-sawn-through shooting-stick Gotcha.

You can't imagine the shambles I encountered when I walked into my first planning meeting. Six months they'd been at it, and the idea of face-painting in the Long Room hadn't even crossed their minds. A bungee-jump wasn't being considered; would you believe they didn't have as much as a contact number for Mr Blobby?

'You people are amateurs,' I stormed.

'Of course we are, Podmore,' replied the field-marshal wearing a Primary Club eyepatch, turning back to watch the rest of *Home and Away*.

You can imagine the amount of frustration Pod's had to suffer, coping with the fuddy-duddies up there in St. John's Wood, NW8 8QN. But one thing they do respect is the history book. Which shows that D.V. Podmore's record in charity cricket is right up there with some of the sport and showbiz greats.

When John Conteh and I went round with the collecting blanket for the Taverners at Southgate in 1982 we'd sent five kiddies to Disneyland before we got halfway round the boundary. And my ninth-wicket partnership of 124 with Roger de Courcy and Nookie Bear against Stragglers of India has never been bettered (though needless to say the Indian Board President Mr Jagmohan Dalmiya has always disputed it, because technically there were three of us).

My proposals for the big day are all within the bounds of good taste and what's more they're guaranteed earners. I've been more than ably assisted as always by my faithful fiancee. The most experienced Di lookalike in the whole of the East Midlands by a sizeable country mile, Jacqui has been on the phone to model agencies all week, bless her, and has managed to assemble a crack squad of fellow professionals to provide the centre-piece of the lunchtime entertainment. While the Red Devils are landing on the pitch, Jacqui and the girls will be sweeping the outfield with metal-detectors.

Hopefully they will be picking up the odd pound coin thrown by generous spectators, and also revealing the winner of the 'Spot the Land-Mine' competition. This will have been buried somewhere in the ground the night before. So all in all it should be feast of fun – like *It's a Royal Knockout*, only without Prince Edward to balls it up.

A surprise contender for the Turner Prize emerges after England lose to West Indies inside three days.

As someone who knows a bit about how to look after himself off the field as well as on it, Pod's been drafted into the ECB scheme set up to give the contracted England cricketers some preparation for life outside the game: marketing, management, playing for Hampshire etc. Plus a full programme of cultural activities. Last weekend, when the lads suddenly found themselves with a couple of free days on their hands after Edgbaston, was the perfect opportunity to broaden a few horizons.

But after trips to Wolverhampton all-weather races and Do-It-All Focus (I'd borrowed George Sharp's OAP card specially, because you get a 10% discount on Sundays) I have to admit I was scratching my head a bit. But then came the phone call from the Chairman: get your arse in the minibus, Pod, and take the boys down to Tate Modern.

His Lordship must have pulled a few strings as we were treated like VIPs, even getting to walk across that new bridge over the Thames which I'd heard was supposed to swing about all over the shop. But from the moment Goughy and Andy Caddick stepped on to it there was no movement whatsoever, it never did a thing. An incident-free crossing, except that Andy Flintoff decked a samosa which Nass chucked to him. He carried on eating it though, swearing it had never touched the ground.

As for the gallery itself, well, I've taken part in some fairly pointless rest day activities in my time as a professional cricketer, but walking round a derelict power station takes the biscuit. Mind you, fantastic space for corporate hospitality. It makes you think – if the place gets as packed as that to see the kind of stuff they've got on display, think how many more you'd attract if you offered decent facilities such as a driving range, food court etc. You could clean up.

Obviously, if you don't charge admission you're always going to get crowd problems. Dave Podmore's not the kind of guy to knock his fellow man, but I have to say that not all the rubbish at Tate Modern was up on the walls. It's no exaggeration to say that of the two hundred and twenty-odd thousand people who were there that morning, me and the lads were the only ones wearing ties with diagonal stripes.

After lunch we all went for a slash and within ten minutes there were photographers, film crews, and reporters asking us for interviews. Apparently we'd pissed in one of the exhibits and the media thought it was some kind of protest, and I suppose the fact that we were neatly dressed in blazers and slacks made us stand out. 'Forget Gilbert and George,' said this posey tosser with a Radio 3 microphone, 'This is the decade of Athers and Stewie and Crofty' etc. etc. – listing the entire squad apart from Ramps.

Suddenly the England squad is not only at the cutting edge of Brit-Art but 13–8 second favourite for the Turner Prize, and the clever money says we can walk it if we manage to dump Hicky. We haven't had many winner's cheques in the England dressing-room of late, and if the Windies series carries on the way it's started we'll have to take anything that comes along.

4

The Ashes Arena

Obviously it's got to be every schoolboy's dream. There you are; Fifth Test at Sydney, fifty thousand people baying for your blood. Beer cans raining down on the England fielders, a couple of guys on the Hill releasing a pig with your name painted on its side. Awesome. All of a sudden – crack – the ball's heading my way, I've stuck a hand out – next thing I know I'm being carried shoulder-high by the lads and Mike Gatting's saying, 'Now look what you've done, Pod. You've only gone and won us the ****ing Ashes.'

I must have run that scene over in my head a thousand times and I still can't believe it never happened. But it didn't and I wasn't picked for the tour and you just have to accept that there are some guys whose faces fit and others who needn't bother. Because there are people running this game who have only ever wanted one thing and that thing I'm sorry to say is Dave Podmore's head on a plate. It's a sad toilet to be honest.

Having said that, I've thoroughly enjoyed my behind-the-scenes roles in recent Ashes clashes. And I think it's fair to say that Pod is now at peace with himself over the fact that he's probably never going to see his name in big letters on the side of an Australian pig. I don't lose sleep any more over the selectorial favouritism enjoyed by certain players such as David Capel, Ian Austin, Joey Benjamin, Chris Cowdrey, Ian Greig and Monte Lynch. Life moves on; and in Pod's case it does so in a spacious yet deceptively grunty Daewoo Esperanto supplied by Ray Poole Daewoo of Hinckley. Wonder what Bully and co are driving these days.

There's no one an Aussie would rather beat than a Pom, and vice versa, but there's a KFC bucketful of mutual respect between the two great cricketing nations. When Jason Gillespie broke my record for most rings in a first-class ear I was the first to shake him by the hand. Likewise when Colin 'Funky' Miller ran out of hair dye after England unexpectedly took a Test into the fifth day, Jacqui and I were there for him. We're one big cricket family really. As Jacqui often says 'Ashes to ashes, dust to dust. If Thommo don't phone you Shane Warne must.'

Australia v England, First Test at Brisbane. Match drawn.

At the end of the day (or lunchtime as it is back home), being on a Test tour seems like a pretty good way of life to Dave Podmore. Not least when you discover a complimentary meat pie thoughtfully placed on your pillow by the hotel staff. And eating it out on my veranda, watching the jelly melt in a most acceptable 44°C heat, I've fallen in love all over again with this big young country.

We've already had a few champagne moments (or Koonawarunga Muddy Landing moments to be strictly accurate). The lads have been bubbling all week, after our historic result in the First Test at the magnificent partially rebuilt Woolongabba Stadium. Getting the draw was tremendous but we were also able to take a lot out of the Gabba game besides. And I don't just mean the 10 litres of sealant, two masonry drills and the orbital sander I managed to get my hands on while the builders were sheltering from the thunderstorms, although obviously that was a big bonus.

The main lesson we learned from the game was that our batsmen are susceptible to intimidation. Allowing Glenn McGrath to get up the pipes of the lower order, not to mention suckering Athers again, was just plain soft. It only goes to confirm what Pod's been banging on about for years, and that is that sledging-wise we're still in the Gentlemen v Players era.

That's why as soon as we got to the WACA yours truly was drafted in to run one of my celebrated sledging clinics to bring the lads up to the necessary level of mouthiness to give the Aussies a fright. My pioneering work in this area has been one of the most successful aspects of the Dave Podmore Academy of Excellence. Let's just say that no youngster has left there without a diploma in kidology.

The net facilities here in Perth have been absolutely brilliant for slagging off so no complaints on that score. Quite reasonably, though, we have refused to practise swearing at one another under floodlights since that was not agreed prior to the start of the tour. The lads have knuckled down well to the rigorous training regimen – with one or two exceptions. Alan Mullally I'm afraid to say can be a right lazy so-and-so: calling McGrath 'Fatty' at Brisbane showed a complete lack of concentration and the boy needed a swift kick up the arse to remind him he's sledging for England.

Gus Fraser doesn't need any lessons in patriotism and even though his swearing isn't as sharp as it was he can still keep up a flow of mild invective for hours. Grand servant to the cause that Gus has been over the years, I personally think that now is the ideal time to give the young Surrey quickie Alex Tudor his head. We've got to look to the future. With Channel 4 running things into the next millennium, bad language is going to be an increasingly important aspect of the game.

Right now the world leaders in this field are the South Africans. Their unorthodox sledging methods – singing 'Kum ba ya' to the incoming batter and asking if he's found the Lord yet – are very off-putting indeed and send most players scurrying back to join their team-mates in the pavilion rather sharpish. We'll see over the next few days how the team shape up. Don't forget they'll be sledging into the teeth of the notorious Fremantle Doctor. This is the wind that blows across Perth and is otherwise known, when the lads have been out for a curry, as the notorious Fremantle Gastro-Enterologist. And historians will tell you that when Mike Brearley led the side in the '70s it was known as the notorious Fremantle Psychotherapist.

The good news is that Jacqui's due to fly out next week. I can't wait: she'll be bringing my costume for the Christmas fancy-dress party. Which means that when she flies home she'll have plenty of room in the trunk to accommodate all the DIY stuff I acquired at the Gabba. It's not been finalised yet what I'll be wearing for the party but I must say the news about the treatment handed out back home to General Augusto Pinochet has set me thinking about some sort of appropriate gesture of support. I've always had a lot of time for 'Gus'. Say what you like about his politics, the guy could certainly fill a stadium.

England v Australia, Second Test: Australia win by seven wickets; Third Test: Australia win by 205 runs.

As usual Stewie had it about right when he said that so far this tour has been a swings-and-roundabouts situation and we've found ourselves on the wrong end of them. Pod would go further and describe it as a switchback ride with no toffee apple at the end of it for the English cricket supporter.

But irregardless of results on the park or the destination of the Ashes, the fans have always been able to comfort themselves with the certainty that when it comes to fancy dress there isn't a team on the planet that can live with us. Christmas Day after Christmas Day, not only in this century but stretching back into the last one, England tourists have established a novelty costume supremacy unrivalled in the annals of sport.

Take a walk through the MCG museum here in Melbourne and you enter a heritage time warp. It's all here – from the crinoline worn by Sir W. G. Grace in the first ever competition to the miniskirt in which Ken Barrington carried all before him as Lulu in 1965/6 (and this after putting Graeme McKenzie to the sword all day on an Adelaide greentop).

Being on their first tour, some of the younger players like Alex Tudor and Peter Such have obviously never taken part in the competition before, so Dave Podmore was entrusted with the task of taking them round the museum to both give them a bit of a history lesson and also point them in the right direction regarding what to wear.

The lads were gobsmacked to discover that, for example, in the era before Kerry Packer revolutionised the game a professional cricketer was expected not only to pay for his costume himself but also to make it. This could take five or six weeks – the entire length of the sea voyage out there – and was the cause of many a notorious contretemps.

Geoff Boycott's absence from the Test arena in the '70s was a case in point. Geoff had sat up night after night applying lacquer to his loon pants only to discover that Mike Denness had also decided to go as David Bowie. The skipper pulled rank with the result that Boycs refused to wear so much as a sequin in anger for three years.

That's not to say that the modern player has it easy. If anything the pressure to produce the goods after the Christmas dinner is greater than ever. Look at Graeme Hick. Brilliant performer at children's party level but quite honestly that Fred Flintstone outfit he turned up in the last time round . . . well, I'm sorry but it was like watching a rabbit in car headlights.

There has probably never been a fancy dress competition as meticulously prepared for as this year's. Nothing was left to chance. Mike Brearley (a famous Bo Derek in his day) had even been roped in as costume psychologist.

The clever money was obviously on Mark Butcher. Butch is a bit of an Audrey Hepburn buff – has been since he was in the Surrey Under-14s. He's got all the skinny lass's videos and knows every word of dialogue from *Breakfast at Tiffany's* (pity the poor sod who has to sit next to him on the plane). Anyway what with the little black dress and the string of pearls, Butch reckoned he had the number one spot sewn up. But he hadn't bargained for Robert Croft putting together one of the most brilliant disguises of all time and coming as a spin bowler.

So, at the end of the day the lads were able to do justice to the very high standards which they set themselves. And to be honest the Aussies never had a price costume-wise. Six Babes and five Terence-Stamp-in-*Priscilla Queen of the Desert*s – talk about clueless. In any case we already knew exactly what they'd be wearing. Mark Waugh tipped us off weeks ago via a contact on the sub-continent.

England v Australia, Fourth Test: England win by 12 runs.

Okay, so we won a Test. Fair enough, if that's the sort of thing that gets everybody excited back home. If it means the lads can come through the Arrivals Channel at Heathrow next month with heads held high, instead of being dumped out of a refrigerated lorry on the M4 slip-road as per usual, well and good.

And as every reader of this column must know by now, the word moaning and groaning doesn't appear in Podmore's Oxford Dictionary (aka the POD). All I'm saying is, you have to look at the Melbourne result in the wider context of the tour as a whole, and what the implications are for the future of the game.

Keeping the guys out on the park for a four-hour session to make up for lost time was just not on. Granted a couple of those punishing hours were spent waiting to see whether or not Steve Bucknor would put his finger up – you know things have gone too far when even an Aussie opener is prepared to walk, rather than hang about forever on the off-chance of the decision going his way.

But you've got to remember that everybody had been out there for something like nine hours the previous day as well. Eating into a touring party's quality time like that is unacceptable, be it in Antigua or Zimbabwe. Even the press boys suffered – Jonathan Agnew pronounced himself choking with emotion at the end of the match. The poor sod had only gone and missed a mammoth sale of laptop sheaths and mouse mats in Melbourne's computer warehouse, or green light, district.

And if Aggers was choked, we were all gutted. Expecting the match to run to schedule – i.e. over by Monday, with no time added on for bad weather – the lads had been looking forward to a decent rest day unwinding with wives etc., followed by a civilised evening at the Gala Opening of Merv's Surf 'n' Turf 'n' Derv garage brasserie (black tie, trousers optional).

Really, something has to be done to change this regulation that keeps both players and press – some no longer in their first flushes – on or around the park till all hours of the night. The 90-over minimum quota is bad enough, especially when you factor in the length of time it takes Gus Fraser to get the ball from one end of the pitch to the other (there was a bin-liner blowing across the outfield at Melbourne which registered quicker on the Sniper speed gun).

Surely common sense tells you that any extra time played on one day should be subtracted from the next day's play, and so on till the game is over. There might be a few grumblers who'll have forked out good money to see five minutes' cricket round day four, but this must happen if the game isn't to become even more of a laughing stock.

On a more positive note, the Test ending early meant that Pod and Jacqui were able to take up Glenn McGrath's kind invitation to spend a relaxing day or two on his charming 450,000-acre spread in the outback. When he's not banging them in at Athers, pig-shooting is the name of the game for the Aussie paceman, and the superb sport we enjoyed made up for our missing the annual Boxing Day meet back home with the Quorn.

I'll tell you something – our friends Mr and Ms Hunt Saboteur wouldn't stand a prayer if Glenn had them in the sights of his trusty 303. And if I was Alan Mullally, I'd think twice before trying to loft him back over his head again.

England lose the series after a controversial decision.

When *Wisden*'s history of this tour comes to be written, you can rest assured there'll be no shortage of highfalutin' verbiage about defining moments, the one in the last Test being the Michael Slater run-out incident affair. Well, before everything gets set in concrete by the scribes, just let Pod tell you what really happened that fateful Monday.

All I was doing was trying to help out a couple of dozen England supporters who'd been unlucky enough not to have tickets when they arrived at Sydney airport. I couldn't very well charge them $750 per ticket with radio sun-hat (batteries not included) if they weren't going to get a decent view of the game. That would be unethical.

So what option did I have but to move the replay camera from where it was, square-on, to a slightly less prominent position in the Herb Adams Meat Pie Stand? The next thing you know, Slats has been given the benefit of the doubt by the third umpire, goes on to notch up a ton and Pod is being given the blame for the lads losing the series.

Anyone who knows me will tell you how ridiculously hurtful and libellous that accusation is. Dave Podmore would die for his country, always assuming the money was right.

Who was it who injured his neck kissing the three lions on his shirt after scoring his maiden run in Test cricket? To be

strictly accurate, it was the attempt to kiss the Tetley's logo on my shoulder that did the long-term damage and, I might add, curtailed a promising international career. The point is that nobody, but nobody, can question Pod's patriotism.

If you're pointing the finger of blame, look no further than Peter Such. It was him who got his arse between the replay camera and the stumps at the crucial moment. And would you believe this was after the lads had spent hours and hours being drilled in correct camera technique by Bob Cottam – he'd even been up at the crack of dawn painting white boxes all over the outfield for the guys to position themselves in. All thrown away in a moment of madness.

You wouldn't catch an experienced pro like Corky not knowing which camera to turn to when he makes one of his (increasingly rare) appeals. But Suchy committed the cardinal schoolboy sin of failing to keep one eye on what I was up to in the stand, as well as watching the game. Until we learn to play for each other as a team, then I'm afraid England will continue to languish in seventh place in the coveted *Wisden* World Rankings.

But there's always got to be a scapegoat, hasn't there? So Pod takes the rap and gets sent home, sat on a plane next to Mike 'Interesting' Atherton, whereas the Australians reward their guys who show a bit of financial initiative. Shane Warne and Mark Waugh put a few calls through to an Indian bookie. Result? They are made captain and vice-captain of the one-day squad. What a wonderful world we live in.

So I arrive back at Heathrow after seven hours of the most boring conversation I've ever had to suffer – if I'd heard one more word about Captain Corelli and his bloody mandarin, Athers' Test career would have been well and truly over. Finally I had no option but to go and spend the rest of the flight sitting next to my fiancee in Economy.

Thankfully Jacqui was in a much more upbeat mood after reading in the papers about the two-for-the-price-of-one Big Mac offer. I tell you, I went through Arrivals faster than an Aussie leggie getting through the England top order.

Of course when we get to the McDonalds at the airport, it's the same old story. Big notice on the window saying they've only run out of beef. Welcome home to Britain, Mr Podmore, and a Happy New 1999 to you too. Being no stranger to injustice, I merely shrugged and went for a Wendy's, but Jacqui went ballistic. 'It's the Hoover offer all over again, Pod,' she wailed. 'We never did get to Orlando, and the suction on the vacuum packs up every time the dogs start moulting.'

Luckily when we got home there was a job offer on the answering machine which proves that Dave Podmore isn't quite ready for the scrapheap as a professional cricketer. There's still a bit of fine-tuning to be done on the car-parking and dressing-room arrangements but I can confidently predict that anyone walking past the poster for the Teletubbies panto in Bromyard will see that as from next week it stars Tinky Winky, Dipsy, Laa-Laa, and – coming in at number four – Pod.

Resavouring the taste of
international recognition.

I got the call from the Chairman of Selectors at the start of the week. After much humming and hawing and general pontification he informed me that in view of the injury situation they had been forced to include Pod in the squad for the First Test. I had to keep pinching myself to check it was really happening.

Sure, I'd have preferred Mr Graveney to have left out the bit about 'with great reluctance', but to be honest when a nod comes your way at my age you want to snaffle it with both hands rather than decking it like an English keeper. So, as I say I've jumped for joy, I've grabbed a lava lamp and run round the lounge with it. I've kissed the digibox and just to make 150% sure of the news I've pinched myself again. Sadly I put a bit too much into the pinch and thereby picked up a niggle, making me at best only 50/50 to start the match.

To add to my woes, as a result of thinking that all my birthdays and Christmases had come at once I overdid it a bit with the trifle, jellies, cake, Christmas pud etc., not to mention hitting myself in the eye with a party-popper. So that meant that along with Ramps, Thorpey, Vaughan and the rest, I found myself up the ladder fitness-wise. Talk about bad luck.

Pod's berth in the middle order went to Usman Afzaal who according to all the media has a reputation as a bit of a street fighter. Fair play to Uzzy and I hope he does ever so well.

Personally I'd back him to fulfil his Stepstone Ambition: to stay at the crease for five minutes. But I could have brought so much more to the party having had fights not just in streets but on dual carriageways, slip-roads and just about every built-up area where parking is an issue. What's more, my religious beliefs allow me to play, and indeed fight, on any day of the week. But you have to put disappointment behind you and move on.

Anyway I don't delude myself that I was ever first choice for the seven spot. I know for a fact that Hicky was ahead of me on Duncan Fletcher's list. As usual the coach had gone to amazing lengths to ensure his enigmatic fellow countryman was ready for his eleventh recall. This time he even went in a darkened van all the way up to Bletchley Park where he'd been granted special permission to use one of the original Enigma machines. Fletch got one of the girls there to type in Hicky's name. A whirr of machinery and what does it come up with? 'Lbw fst bll. Ddnt mv his ft.' You can't argue with that kind of technology.

Quite a few other ex-England players' eyes lit up once they saw the mounting injury list for the current Test. When the word got round that Duncan Fletcher was going to be at Trent Bridge on a scouting mission to watch the 'Masters' match against Australia last Sunday, Graham Gooch for one took his preparations very seriously indeed. He booked himself in for one of Steve Bull's hypnotherapy sessions. Goochie transported himself back in time all right but unfortunately it wasn't to Lord's in 1990 where he got his 300. It was to Edgbaston in 1975 where Jeff Thomson got him out first ball, and guess what happens? Thommo got him out for another duck. We still have much to learn about the workings of the human brain even with a hair transplant on it.

Looking down the card for the match, top scorer against the Aussie Masters was Derek Randall, with his cartwheels and his refreshing bloody attitude. Arkle's never been one of Pod's favourites, ever since I put all the hard-earned money I'd got for my free John Player League fags on laughing boy getting nought in the Centenary Test 25 years ago. I'm sorry, but that temperament is just not suited to today's ultra-professional cricket betting market. He's that carefree he'd probably tell you the weather forecast for nothing.

Steve Waugh's side: the brainiest Australians ever?

It seems the whole Aussie nation is up in arms and crying over its breakfast cereal and skimmed koala milk, just because of some extremely sensible remarks made in these columns by the British Lion Austin Healey. And now Dave Podmore too has been warned not to be offensive, and mind his p's and q's (also r's for roo-shaggers) when discussing the sensitive termite-munchers from the former penal colonies. After all, they're our guests.

I'm happy to oblige, because the Australian cricket team is a country mile in advance of the Wallabies when it comes to grey matter matters. There isn't a 'plod' or 'plank' among this lot, in fact I've seen Michael Slater go through a crossword with a pets theme quicker than Stephen Fry. Much of the Aussies' mental ascendancy is down to their remarkable captain Steve Waugh.

Tugger's brainwave was that each and every ocker should turn up in the dressing room before a match with an inspiring line of prose or poetry. The idea came to him apparently on day one of the tour when he spotted a shop called Borders in Oxford Street, and naturally enough decided to give it a go. He liked what he saw, and since then his boys have spent every spare moment looking for suitable quotes to stick on their Post-It notes, the upshot being that now they not only play hard but they recite hard too.

'It's the best of times for us mate, but the worst of times for you, you pommy bastard,' was just one of the upmarket sledges that Channel 4's stump mike picked up on Thursday from Shane Warne (or 'Somerset' Warne as he now likes to be known). Luckily Mike Atherton was out there in the middle, and was able to use his ton of Oxbridge experience to come back with 'It droppeth as the gentle dew from heaven, mate,' every time Mark 'Evelyn' Waugh decked a sitter.

Though some of Caretaker Captain 'Corelli' Atherton's nicknames for our own lads haven't been too clever, to be honest. Stewie really likes being Sir Walter Scott for some reason, but calling Andy Caddick Virginia Woolf is a massive risk given his already suspect temperament. And expecting Ramps to get us out of jail after he'd been dubbed Jeffrey Archer was just asking for trouble.

Pod's nothing if not an optimist, however, and I still think we can turn this series round. To me there's a big question mark about the Australians' commitment and patriotism. Who was it who recently turned down the opportunity to captain his country against the Windies because of, boo-hoo, a poorly buttock? Step forward Mister Steve Waugh, that is if you're able to move without a nurse and a Stairmaster. No offence, Auberon, but if people over here pulled a sickie every time we picked up an arse niggle the place would grind to a halt. Channel 4 would go off the air for starters.

England v Australia, Fourth Test at Headingley. England win by six wickets.

Once again the England boys have shown the Australians how the game of cricket should be played, and sent them scurrying back to their poetry books in disarray and searching desperately for inspiration. Dave Podmore can offer them this time-saving advice: look no further than Butch's post-match interview, when Aggers asked how he'd spent the lunch interval: 'I sat in the shower, had a cup of coffee and a couple of cigarettes.'

Not 'I knocked off another Shakespeare play over a salad,' you notice. Pod thinks there's a lesson in those fags, and it seems the selectors have finally learnt it albeit nearly too late. It's no accident that the side for the Oval includes Tuffers – England's leading practitioner of the art and, next to Mrs Thatcher and Ken Clarke, just about the finest ambassador smoking could wish for.

So the myth of the invincible Aussie machine has been well and truly exploded, and not before time. There's been a lot of verbiage about them taking the game to a new level – but it's a new level of boredom as far as I'm concerned. Talk about personality by-passes. I had more laughs at Corky's latest benefit do than with this lot, and there was just me and the weatherman from Radio Chesterfield there.

Their other halves aren't much better. Jacqui offered to take the sheilas for a girls' day out – a relaxing afternoon at the factory shop, followed by an evening watching some strapping

Aussie lads get their kit off in a saucy show called The Puppetry of the Penis. But oh no, they were la-di-dahing it off to Stratford-on-bloody-Avon for the afternoon – on a train would you believe – where as Jacqui says there isn't even an Accessorize, let alone a Kookai.

All of which makes for a pretty dull bunch of tourists. And it's not just their fixation with poetry and modern architecture, ballet etc. – they're cricket-obsessed too. Dave Podmore has got news for you cobbers – the late Sir Don Bradman has already named his all-time World XI to take on Mars. You weren't in it. That particular convict ship has sailed, so lighten up.

And another thing. It's bad enough they come here expecting to take our Ashes. Now they're taking our newspaper columns too. Don't get me wrong: I've nothing against stinging the London media bosses for a few grand a week, do it myself regularly. But rather than making a quick call from the car in the normal way, some of these Aussies actually write their own stuff. God knows how long that must take.

Personally I give it five minutes max, then it's 'Sorry fellas, I'm going under a bridge. Speak next week.' But to see an international sportsman at the peak of his earning powers bent over a Sylvine exercise book, pencil in hand with his tongue pitifully sticking out as he tries to get his letters right – well, it debases the game of cricket.

On the players' balcony during the last Test I even saw a couple of the Aussie lads' lips moving as they ploughed through the reissue of Mike Brearley's *The Art of Captaincy*. It may be 20 years old but it's still the bible as far as most of them are concerned – you've only got to look at Shane Warne's flares to see the awe in which they regard the Ayatollah's views.

Didn't do them much good laying the Headingley hoodoo to rest, did it? In other words if they spent a bit less time writing their columns, reading books etc. and a bit more smoking and trying to do justice to *The Puzzler Summer Special*, they might have achieved the 5–0 whitewash that Pod stuck 500 hard-earned notes on.

5

The Motivation Arena

All the motivation I've ever needed to go out and do a job for England is those three little lions and the Vodafone logo on my chest. Put it this way, if pulling on an England sweater, or acrylic relaxing fleece, doesn't give you a big red, white and blue lump in your throat then you're either sick in the head or born abroad, and either way I'd have very little time for you.

This is not to say Dave Podmore don't appreciate the value of modern motivational techniques. When I was at Derbyshire the committee sent us off to undergo a series of intense hypnotherapy sessions designed to help a player to dig deep into his subconscious psyche to find his strongest game. My strongest game turned out to be three-card brag, and I've been taking money off the lads regularly every time it rains ever since. So Pod keeps an open mind on matters psychological.

Another case in point: I have no medical training whatsoever, but I seem to have this knack, call it a gift if you like, of bringing kiddies out of comas. It dates back to my last-but-one benefit season, when during a lunch interval I accidentally dropped the big cardboard cheque that was being presented to me by a youngster from an orphanage. It landed on his head and the next thing I knew he was being rushed into Derby General, spark out. Sitting by the little mite's bed after close of play I whispered in his ear all the things he was missing, such as his hero taking a tidy two-for just after tea. His little eyelids flickered and I tiptoed from the room. Job done.

Before long I was getting so many requests from hospitals throughout the Trent Health Authority that I had to record wake-up messages on to cassettes. David Lloyd was England manager at the time and Bumble bought a couple in desperation after the disappointing way the lads had responded to his Winston Churchill tapes and the inspirational video of the bombing of Dresden.

I wouldn't go so far as to say that bringing kiddies out of comas is the new rock and roll, but make no mistake about it, there's a very big wad indeed to be made out of the mysterious workings of the human brain.

I commend to you my writings on this most fascinating of subjects . . .

England seek to gain the psychological edge over Australia prior to the Fourth Test.

An excellent decision by David Lloyd and the other management honchos to set up this weekend's motivation and bonding session at Headingley. But I have to say it was very disappointing for me personally that Will Carling's company Insights got the nod to host the event when they could have had Dave Podmore's unique 'Podivation' seminar which has been putting so many executive bums on red-velour stacking chairs recently. If there's a Moat House within easy reach of the M25 where we haven't held an inspirational proactivity weekend I'd very much like to know where it is.

Why would anyone want to listen to a poncey rugger bugger when they could have had Barry Sheene and the darts world's Keith Deller giving them the goods about personal goal prioritisation? It comes a bit more pricey admittedly but you're getting the pure drug with a guy like that, plus a mid-morning cup of Rombouts and a complimentary Podivation document wallet for £499 plus VAT all in (afternoon tea and paint-gun cartridges not included).

Premier athletes such as Will and myself have had to face up to the realisation that no way can you subject your body to the demands of top-level sport indefinitely (I confess I felt a tell-tale twinge on Monday while putting together a handy 9 in the AON

Risk game against Durham). So it's only common sense to have a few quid put by for the sad day when you have to hang up your boots (especially if you've put a substantial chunk of your hard-earned benefit money into the only building society that decides not to go public – thank you very much the Dorchester & Swanage).

In addition you're doing a public service by handing down a ton and a half of accumulated sporting experience which Team England so urgently needs. Sad to say this has led to some small-mindedness among colleagues jealous that the name Pod is spoken of with reverence wherever middle-managers gather. Only this week I'm convinced I heard a quite unnecessary chant coming from my own dressing room:

> 'Who's had all the pie-charts?
> Who's had all the pie-charts?
> Poddy, Poddy, you fat bastard,
> You've had all the pie-charts.'

I sincerely hope the lads benefit from their weekend with Will's organisation, though if he's planning to take them up a mountain in Land Rovers I hope to Christ I don't get the nod at the last minute. I wouldn't fancy driving blindfolded with one of our bowling attack doing the navigating. Still, it's all about finding yourself, isn't it? Dare to excel, lads.

Pod's Footnote

Australia won by an innings and 61 runs, but congratulations to Will Carling on a very successful weekend indeed. No hard feelings whatsoever about that, or the time when him and his missis got the nod ahead of Jacqui and myself for the Quorn savoury bake advert. All I'd say about that is who's still slipping her fella's dinner in the microwave – Julia or Jacqui?

England crash to sixth consecutive Ashes defeat after looking to the Orient for inspiration.

Okay, so there's got to be a scapegoat. And Pod's not about to desert the sinking ship by not claiming at least some of the responsibility. But I want it to go on record that when I first introduced the idea of Feng Shui as a way of turning round the Ashes series, Bumble, Grav and the rest of the England management were well up for it. I've even got the ECB Consultant's blazer and tie to prove it.

As most people reading a paper like this are probably aware, Feng Shui is an ancient Chinese Oriental art of getting a result by putting things in special places. I hadn't come across it before myself, but then Jacqui arrived in Adelaide and she was full of it, having read an article in *Bella* magazine while she was at the beautician's.

Not two days after rearranging the kitchen to harness the natural forces of the universe a bit better, she won £75 on a scratchcard. Admittedly, she then had to go back to Country Cuticles and spend another £30 getting her nail repaired, but the point I made to Graham Gooch is that Jacqui was up on the day. And let's face it, after Perth he was ready to try anything.

It's not as if the lads didn't put the work in. We spent hours shifting all the kit round in the dressing-room to affirm our life-stations: Goughy laid out his socks and boots pointing east,

Creepy filled his shin pads with crystals and even Stewie entered into the spirit by putting a scented candle at each end of his vortex, though personally I think he was taking on too much.

Things got a bit fraught when Dean Headley tried to create a zone of transition by hanging a mobile from the ceiling above his peg. He didn't realise that the mobile was supposed to be one of those birds-and-fish jobs that move about in the wind. By not getting up to his phone in time, Deano found out later, he missed out on the chance of snapping up the late Doug Wright's allotment.

And of course, what Feng Shui doesn't legislate for is the Aussies bringing on Colin Miller to knock the top order over. Then Hicky's centre of prosperity somehow got turned into a centre of having a big wipe outside off-peg. Result? Ancient Chinese score of 0. And it transpired that the rest of the tail thought they were doing Kung Fu anyway, a game which is over very quickly indeed.

So the position now is that we're looking for ways to keep the series alive. Something to get the crowds back and placate those sad tossers who've spent their life savings coming out here to see a genuine contest. The ground authorities are doing their best, and those lunchtime games of Chase the Sheila are all very well for the locals, but the fact remains that we're not very good at it. We seem to be able to get the Sheila into our hands but then let her go again, unfortunately. It's not that we don't care. We've just stopped believing we can catch her.

But there is one suggestion that Pod's got quite a bit of time for. There's a campaign been going on round here for the last few weeks called 'Bring Back the Don'. The idea being that instead of

95

some of the other guys knocking on the door – the Blewetts, the Lehmanns and the Bevans – the Australian selectors should give the nod to Bradman, to help the old boy get those elusive four runs that would give him a Test average of 100.00. One crack through the covers ought to do it – his eyesight might not be what it was, but Sir Donald should be able to climb into Crofty without too much bother. And even if he gets himself caught, you can always rely on an Aussie third umpire to get him off the hook.

The England selectors might do well to consider a few legendary names from our own Hall of Fame. Peter May, for example. The guy may no longer be technically alive, but you can't tell Pod that he wouldn't put up a better show than Hicky or Creepy (there'd probably be a bit more movement of the feet as well) while Ramps plays a dead bat at the other end.

Sure, it might throw the record books into disarray, but that's quite likely to happen anyway now that the ACB are considering recommendations that future matches between England and Australia should no longer be regarded as first-class.

The Chairman of Selectors draws a lesson from the result of the general election.

Pod was minding his own business at home the other night, watching *The World's Worst People-Carrier Accidents* on BBC Choice, when the phone went. A quick check of the international clocks on the living-room wall told me it was unlikely to be a business associate on the subcontinent, wanting an update on weather and pitch conditions at Old Trafford, so I let it ring.

When the programme showed a people-carrier crash I'd seen before (had caused, actually), I listened to the message. It was the elegant public-school tones of someone not a million miles from the Powers That Be. 'We're in the poo, Pod,' the voice said. I could tell from the slight rustle of moustache against the mouthpiece and faint chinking of gold chain that this was none other than the Chairman of Selectors. 'We need some expert help dealing with the "c" word.' My mind raced. Cars? Curry?

'Complacency,' the message went on. 'You may not have noticed, but we're in serious danger of beating Pakistan at Old Trafford and thereby winning five Test series in a row. What's needed is something or someone to put Team England on its mettle for the Ashes.'

I hadn't noticed the cricket much, actually. Most of my spare time had been spent in the common sense arena, supporting William Hague as he gutsed it out to save the pound. When you're out on the stump (and often *with* the stump, some of those bus queues can turn pretty ugly) there are more important things to do than watch Goughie doing himself an injury as he twists round to check his mph on the speed gun.

Getting the nod from Conservative Central Office last month seemed like it was going to be a seriously big feather in the cap of Pod 'n' Jacqui Image Consultants. After our success with the Lutterworth by-pass presentation, seeing off those tossers from the environmental lobby, word had got round that our little company was hot-wired to the heartbeat of Middle England. No offence to Seb Coe, but as an adviser to a potential future Prime Minister he was never pulling up any trees. Rolling about on a judo mat is not, I am afraid, the way to claw back the vote of the ordinary guy in the street who enjoys his darts and his dog-fighting of a Saturday night.

Ffion and Jacqui clicked straight away. Look at the way Mrs Hague stood there for weeks on end radiating attractiveness and only using her mouth for grinning purposes. Obviously she was in the expert hands of a PR big-hitter, someone who knows how to sell the image of an exciting new product, be it a miracle potato cutter or a political party. If only Jacqui could have convinced the Tory lass to put her hair up they'd have been back in power and the Euro would be dead in the water. As it is this time next week we'll probably all be driving on the right.

And I would have to hold my hand up and say I didn't do myself justice in the nets, coaching Haguey. If Dave Podmore is known for nothing else it's (a) having a reasonable thirst and (b) having equally reasonable views on immigration. I'm all for sledging our friends from the sub-continent and having a few beers afterwards, or at the beginning and in the middle come to that, but even I couldn't keep pace with the leader of Her Majesty's Opposition (or, by the time you read this, something in the City).

But one door closes and another one opens, etc. My long association with losing sides obviously planted the thought in David Graveney's mind that I was just the guy to combat the atmosphere of complacency creeping into the England camp amid the current landslide of Test victories. So I had a session with the lads and showed them how we used to do it back in the '80s under the regimes of May and Dexter.

In other words, play your natural game and don't worry too much about the result, or if you deck a few slip catches at vital moments or lose eight wickets in a session. You can always blame crap umpiring decisions or the alignment of the planets or not having Hicky in the side – anything really. It's only a bloody game, for Christ's sake. Result, atmosphere of complacency dispatched from the dressing room, arrivederci over-confidence, bring on the Aussies. Thank you very much Pod, pop your invoice in the post.

Australia are on course for their seventh successive Ashes victory despite their outmoded Oriental inspiration techniques.

Dave Podmore is all for pushing the envelope when it comes to sports strategy. But you have to make sure that when you do it you push the aforesaid envelope under the right hotel door. Unfortunately the Aussie manager and gaffe-meister John Buchanan failed to observe this simple rule, accidentally delivering the so-called sayings of a certain Mr Sun Tzu into the hands of someone who, not being an Australian cricketer, had a sense of humour and leaked it to the media.

Besides, if you really want to get a bit of team spirit going there are far better things to put under hotel doors than copies of the works of Sun Tzu Esq. There's the joke fax from reception saying your kids have been eaten by sharks, or the Naughty Fido novelty with a hot kettle poured over it to create that fresh steaming effect. It's all about bonding.

In any case, it's a very high-risk policy to assume an international cricketer is going to be in the hotel room he's supposed to be in. And this was where manager Buchanan was a victim of his own cleverness. He'd been banging on so much about the Aussies needing to move up a level now they'd set a benchmark, that by the time he'd got the photocopying done the lads had got the wrong end of the stick and checked into another set of rooms

one floor up. Result: dingo doo-doo hitting the air conditioning big-style.

The words of ancient wisdom in question only go to show how far the Australians lag behind us in motivation techniques, as in everything else. I used all that Chinese warlord bollocks in my management seminars way back in the '90s. If you'd played for England a couple of times and could work a flip chart without picking up a niggle it was a licence to print money. You wouldn't believe the number of sales reps prepared to fork out £500 a head to listen to the thoughts of Sun Tzu in my 'Podivation' sessions and, what's more, part with another 40 notes so they could listen to the cassette on the M25 going home. Confucius he say it like taking banana fritter from a baby.

I don't know who first made up the name Sun Tzu. I've got a feeling it was one of the commentators on Sky Sports about five years ago when they were showing rugby league in the middle of the night and trying to make it interesting. Before long the darts, golf and moto-cross communities got in on the warlord act and suddenly there wasn't a Moat House Conference Suite in the country which didn't have 50 blokes taking notes about 'Occupying The Dispersive Ground' and enjoying an ancient Chinese complimentary packet of digestive biscuits. Oh yes, he was bloody good to us, was Sun Tzu-ey.

But you can't stand still in Test cricket (unless you're Banger Trescothick facing Dizzy Gillespie). Team England has been typically proactive in its morale-building programme while the Aussies are still playing catch-up. The ECB's latest brainwave is to borrow the quota system used in South Africa and Zimbabwe which encourages ethnic minorities. It's early doors still and we haven't yet found a 17-year-old schoolkid like Hamilton Masakadza who can score a century on his Test debut, but we have got Crofty who's Welsh. So fingers crossed he can do the business at Trent Bridge and follow it up with a result at what Sun Tzu calls 'The Desperate Ground' (Headingley).

6

The Ten Grand in a Bin-liner behind the Portaloo Arena

Like all right-thinking cricketers Dave Podmore was literally shocked to his marrows when the news first came through that Mark Waugh and Shane Warne had accepted around £2000 each from an Indian bookmaker to provide routine information about pitch and weather conditions. I said at the time that it was an absolute disgrace, a mire from which cricket would take years to recover, and I have had no cause to revise my views since then.

Personally, I always ask for at least five grand plus a monkey for my out-of-pocket expenses. Those Bombay bookies will usually throw in a holiday in Goa too if you do a decent one-phone-call-no-fuss job. But 2K, I ask you. By accepting less than 50% below the going rate Warney and Waughey sold their fellow professionals down the river. Not only was it 'naïve and stupid', as they admitted, they were taking bread out of guys' mouths.

Apparently Waugh Junior trousered an extra thousand dollars for providing details of the long-range weather outlook.

But even if you allow for inflation and convert it using the current exchange rate it still only comes to £2,786.81-odd. Now if you're a single mother sitting reading this in a container lorry, I suppose it might seem like a reasonable rate of pay. But for an international sportsman at the peak of his weather-forecasting powers . . . well, Dave Podmore doesn't need to spell it out. It's pitiful.

As we all know now, this was but the tip of the most shameful iceberg in Test history. Cast your mind back, if you will, to Nagpur, 19 December 2000. Herschelle Gibbs and Henry Williams entered into a gentlemen's agreement with Mr 'Banjo' Cassim of Cape Town and Mr Sanjeev Chawla of Southall; Henry undertook to bowl complete dogfood at the start of the match while Herschelle agreed to whack one up in the air and get himself caught early doors. They chose to do neither. In reneging on the agreement they spat on a thousand-odd years of cricketing tradition. If the sacred bond of trust between a cricketer and his turf accountant breaks down, the betting element of the game will go down the toilet and a vital source of income at grassroots level will vanish forever.

The following insider's account of the mire as it unfolded month by month is probably the most comprehensive yet published. It is a matter of deep regret that Dave Podmore has been forced to reproduce it for so little money.

Reflections from 'Down Under'
on professional cricketers'
living standards.

Lying in the bath this morning watching the 'Hair Dinkum' frequent-use shampoo suds disappearing the wrong way down the plughole, I was reflecting on how the lot of the pro has changed in my time. When I first came into the game I thought betting on the spread meant what kind of Shippam's you'd get during the tea interval. But it's amazing how quickly you learn when you're young.

When I was at Derbyshire, Notts and Leicester I had a mutually rewarding relationship with Geo. Salmon (Turf Accountant) of Ilkeston. Over the years I provided George, God rest his soul, with comprehensive coverage not just of weather and pitch details but everything from who'd performed in the nets to who'd been on the nest the night before a game.

For this work I received an honest day's pay – plus a port-and-stilton presentation pack in Pod's stocking come Christmas. It's fair to say that if I hadn't had this extra income I would not have been able to enjoy my current lifestyle e.g. a nice house, five dogs and an attractive fiancee who hopefully won't have to call me again in the middle of the night because she's forgotten that you have to waggle the steering wheel before you can turn the ignition key.

You certainly can't make that kind of money from county

cricket. I saw the writing on the wall early in my career when I witnessed my old mentor Ted Crapp deliberately treading on his stumps on the last day of the season, thereby settling the Championship. His reward? Five Woodbines. Something had to change. And Pod likes to think he's played his part in improving the lot of the modern player by forging strong links between the pro at grassroots level and the bookmaker on the sub-continent.

Sure, there were objections from the diehards, as there always are when someone comes up with a fresh idea, but my scale of charges for predicting and indeed influencing the outcome of matches is now widely accepted throughout the first-class game. And I hear it's on the table at the next ICC meeting. The charges range from £25,000 to swing a World Cup Final down to £25 to get a result against the Combined Universities. Increasingly popular among the odds-laying fraternity is Pod's Platinum Service: nobble two umpires, get the third free.

The way I see it, I'm a bit like the National Trust – preserving the game for the next generation. At any rate that's what I told the kiddy outside the ground at Luton that day we lost controversially to Essex inside four hours. 'Say it ain't so, Pod,' he wept to his hero. 'It bloody is,' I retorted, 'and what's more you're a very lucky lad to have seen a batsman get out Hit the Ball Twice in both innings. The odds against that happening must be 100–1.' And they were too.

The big mistake the Australian Cricket Board made was in trying to cover up the whole Waugh/Warne affair. They thought they'd get away with it because although one or two guys had seen the money going into Warnie's hand, no one had been able to spot how it came out. The trouble is we're now in a situation whereby we don't know which international matches have been fixed and which haven't. Some of them might not have been fixed at all. We just don't know. Where does that leave the record books? You might well ask. It's quite possible that the coveted *Wisden* World Rankings will have to be thrown out of the window because as they stand they're completely meaningless.

One thing's for sure, the Pakistanis must be laughing up their sleeves. The crocodiles in the Aussie media have been so busy snapping at their own arses this week that they've missed the real story on Aamir Sohail's absence from the Test against Zimbabwe. The reason he went AWOL was he was legging it across Lahore to get some of the 13-8 on Alex Tudor appearing in our Christmas fancy-dress party as Princess Diana.

A misunderstanding leads to hopes of a roving commission

I knew something was up when the skipper told me an hour before the match that he wanted me to open the bowling. Usually Dave Podmore's role is to come on in mid-dig, take the pace off the ball and try to keep the runs under 10 an over. True, it hadn't been all that successful as a plan, but as for 'Open the bowling, Pod,' – well, it stank. Everyone on the circuit knows I'm not at my most accurate just after a meal break.

We were due to field second (the toss had been fixed weeks before) and as far as I was concerned the plan was for the oppo to lose early wickets then stage a recovery and squeak it at the death with a couple of scampered leg-byes. But all of a sudden it's 'Have a burst with the new cherry and don't worry if you spray it around a bit.'

Normally I'd have expected to bowl less than 35 wides in my five overs but, what with a ball that must have come straight from the Lord's shop and an umpire who was obviously in on it too, it dawned on me that there might be one or two rupees going on the total number of extras.

The next time I see the skipper he's in a brand new Pajero with torsion control and airbags coming out its arse. It's the deception of it all I can't stomach. He's trying to deny Podgate but he knows he's implicated, I know it, and what's more Geo.

Salmon Jnr. (Turf Accountant) of Chesterfield knows it too. The spire's not the only thing that's bent there.

Match fixing, illegal gambling, weather forecasting, call it what you like, it's all part of the game. But it has to be properly controlled and we have to do more to bring the loose cannons into line than supergluing Chris Lewis's Calvin Klein briefs to his peg. That's just cosmetic really. Nor does giving Messrs Malik and ur-Rehman the slap on the wrist of a life ban go far enough. Pod says remove Pakistan from world cricket right now, together with any other countries who can't keep their players' mouths shut. Admittedly, there's a danger there won't be any international cricket at all for the foreseeable future, but on the other hand it would open up the *Wisden* rankings and give England a shout at moving up a bit.

I'm glad to hear that ECB czar Lord MacLaurin is planning to appoint a figure of substance with a wide-ranging brief to get to the bottom of this global scandal. Somebody's going to get a tan out of this, and with all my wealth of experience I see no reason why it shouldn't be me. And my fiancee Jacqui, obviously. Dave Podmore will be available for the man-of-substance nod, because I know for a fact I'm not going to be picked for the forthcoming series against the Windies, or for the one-day triangular tournament. Which, I'm reliably informed, is going to be very close indeed, especially the first floodlit match at Bristol. I can give you the bowling figures if you like.

I suspect that his lordship is also talking sound common sense when he says that the game in some parts of the world is in the grip of the Mafia. It's surely no accident that the old guy who everyone mysteriously voted for as *Wisden*'s Cricketer of the

Century calls himself 'The Don'. And just look at Mark Ramprakash's concrete boots – you can't tell me there's no mob connection there.

England tourists come under close scrutiny in Pakistan.

I can't say too much about this right now but Dave Podmore will in fact be central to the forthcoming series albeit in an undercover capacity. You may have heard about the initiative taken by General Zia, appointing a secret agent to spy on any of the Pakistan lads who might be taking bungs and back-handers. Well, it wasn't long before the ECB cottoned on to the idea, especially in view of the almost supernatural improvement shown by England this season – you can't tell me it's entirely kosher. And who better to undertake this espionage mission than someone whose career batting average is not unadjacent to .007?

I shall be working incognito, naturally, in a variety of guises which for obvious reasons must remain just that. If you're a touring international cricketer you tend to spend a fair bit of time off the park dressing as a woman. I've adopted identities as diverse as Diana Ross and Bet Lynch so I'm highly qualified for the job as well as being aware that it's not without its risks – Javed Miandad swears blind it wasn't him who put chilli powder in my blusher on the '87 tour but why was he there with his camcorder if not?

The merest hint of a conversation with a bookmaker will be instantly picked up by specially adapted tins of corned beef and winter vegetable soup with sausage. These recording devices are the brainchild of the ECB gizmo czar, who's also come up with a cyanide samosa and an exploding CD of 'The Hottest Themes from TV Commercials – Ever (Volume 3)'.

I can't pretend my months underground aren't going to be hard on Jacqui. When she asked what hotel I'd be staying in I could only say, 'If I told you, love, I'd have to kill you.' Though she'll be more than kept busy running my fan club. Coming up with a new name for starters – 'The Pod-O-Philes' is just asking to have your front door kicked in.

A confession is extracted under duress.

You wonder sometimes if there is ever going to be an end to the meddling of the boys in blue, and I don't mean the Gloucester Gladiators. It's not enough that they victimise a motorist on the M62 for taking an important business call on his mobile while taking an equally important swig of his Sunny Delight – now we've got the report on so-called corruption in cricket by Lord 'Bev' Condon.

Dave Podmore would have to hold his hand up and say I might have inadvertently made things worse by giving Bev the impression that the game was so bent that a murder could have taken place in South Africa. The fact is our discussion dragged on and on – we'd been sat in Coffee Republic for over two hours with only flapjacks on offer and, as any nutritional expert will tell you, a cricketer's performance is bound to be affected be it on the park or in a police interrogation situation.

So you could hardly blame me for saying I could murder a curry. He's got a bit of a one-track mind, has Lord Plod, and he got hold of the idea that I wanted to murder A. Kourie, the slow left armer from Transvaal, which is very far from the truth. I did in fact have a bit of a run-in with Alan Kourie on one of my many visits to the veldt in the early '80s (before that superb country went down the crapper) but it was over a free sponsor's putting glove at Sun City – nothing whatsoever to do with match fixing.

But to be honest I was that hungry by then I let Bev think what he wanted, and being a copper he puts two and two together and makes 77 pages saying the game is rotten to the core. On the positive side I cleaned up on the spread, buying at 25–30 pages after a tip-off from a mole at the printers, but that's beside the point.

Sure, there may have been the odd bit of naughtiness in certain parts of the world where they've seen fit to remove Her Majesty's head from the stamps. It's been officially catalogued in *Wisden* about how Hansie Cronje's South Africans rolled over after being bribed with biltong by 'Banjo' Cassim (Turf Accountant) of Cape Town. We've seen how the Indian boys displayed similar lack of backbone when Mr Cassim lured them off the straight and narrow by hauling buckets of biryani on a rope up to the dressing room.

Pod's here to tell you that this could never happen in this country. I've eaten with most of our centrally contracted players and I can categorically state that, with the possible exception of Mike Atherton, none of them will so much as touch a dish unless they've seen a photo of it in the menu first.

As regards the allegations of drug smuggling in team baggage – heroin in the batting gloves etc., I'm sorry but that is a pile of the purest pants. Under the new dynamic Duncan Fletcher regime there's only one thing that goes in those kitbags apart from kit and that's practical jokes for the omniportant pre-match bonding sessions. The idea that there'd be any room in guys' gloves for anything but treacle and frozen prawns is laughable. Likewise only an over-zealous jobsworth copper could possibly mistake itching powder from the joke shop outside

Trent Bridge for cocaine from the primary school down the road.

Bev Condon bangs on big-style about the climate of apathy, cynicism and silence in the game. Dave Podmore deplores this gratuitous sideswipe at the County Championship. A cricketer's career is a short one – I'll have had barely 30 years by the time I decide to hang up my E-zee Breethe adhesive nostril expander. So who can blame us for trying to maximise our earnings in the short term?

You may say I was naïve to accept ten grand's worth of rupees in a bin-liner behind a portaloo at Jesmond in 1997 but no one was more surprised than me when Fat Mo turned out not to be a journalist from a quality Sunday broadsheet after all. Anyway, all I'd revealed was the unremarkable if not downright dull information that our fourth seamer (Spamhead) would come on to bowl at the pavilion end at exactly twelve minutes past five and deliver his second ball in a viking helmet and pink wig (supplied by the twelfth man, D. V. Podmore running on from the long-off boundary). It had no effect whatsoever on the outcome of the game in any case. We'd long since failed to reach agreements with Lancashire after the time they refused to knock off the winning runs by six o'clock so the lads could get back in time to watch *Thunderbirds*.

The upshot is that Condony's recommended a global network of Security Managers, one with every team to stamp out this harmless source of pin money. Still, swings and roundabouts. They've got to recruit them from somewhere and who better than soon-to-be-retired county cricketers? Sounds like blazers and suntans all round again – plus business-class travel and complimentary headsquares for the ladies. Evenin' all.

7

The Touring Arena

There's nothing to beat going round the world at someone else's expense, especially if you don't have to do a stroke of work to earn the privilege. But if you aren't lucky enough to be on the fringes of the England team, Pod recommends getting yourself a gig as a tour party host. True, there's a certain amount of singing for your supper involved, but it's usually in an uproarious karaoke situation.

And keeping yourself there or thereabouts almost certainly guarantees an eventual place in the England team, as there's bound to be a broken finger or three, not to mention some of the guys going down with Delhi belly – often, when it comes to touring the sub-continent, as soon as their selection has been announced.

In Dave Podmore's opinion the Guvnor of touring destinations is Barbados, no question. The island has just about everything a professional cricketer needs to prepare for a crucial Test match, except perhaps a proper dog track. Close your eyes and you could imagine you're in Chelmsford on a Benson & Hedges quarter-final day. Open them and you think you are, what with 7000 beetroot-faced Brits stripped to the waist and cheering for the Old Country.

In short, it's paradise. The superbly-equipped Pirate Sam's Paradise Motel, to be exact. When the wind's whipping in off the Atlantic you can always take refuge in the Smugglers Bar with its state-of-the-art Games Cove. One bloke from the *Telegraph* on the last tour did so well on the Lucky Doubloons fruit machine that he paid for his nipper's first year at Bedales.

Of course no totally unsolicited testimonial to Barbados would be complete without a mention of the all-day excursion round the island on board the good ship Jolly Roger. This convivial but at the same time educational voyage takes about as long as a day's play except that the drinks interval lasts the whole three sessions.

The great danger of going abroad with England is allowing the cricket to dominate everything. Hopefully the following extracts from Pod's diary of the most recent Caribbean campaign will show that there's more to touring than just the sight of Nass and the lads on a beach, running backwards in their shorts.

England v West Indies, First Test, Sabina Park. England 17-3 (match abandoned).

All that careful preparation; all that dedicated build-up to the big day itself . . . and all swept away in the space of an hour. But when you get the nod to go on a tour of the Windies you have to take the rough with the smooth.

Being in the firing line as a celebrity host abroad is in Dave Podmore's humble opinion an even harder job than being out there on the park. Believe me, those who have paid upwards of seven grand to travel with Ian Treen Tours of Tamworth take no prisoners – though I did hear rumours of one Club Fred Rumsey courier being locked in his hotel room. He was not let out until everybody had received their welcome pack of complimentary driftwood for the beach cricket.

It is a tragedy for all concerned, because the general consensus is that this is the strongest party of Caribbean tour operators to set foot on the azure sands for many years. Ian Treen himself played a few times for the Leicester Second XI in the early '80s (which is where our paths crossed) to qualify as a first-class travel agent.

Just look at the talent in depth we have out here. What schoolboy does not dream of sharing a couple of post-match rum punches with the likes of 'Deadly' Derek Underwood, Alan Oakman, John Price and David Capel? Who better to entertain you with a potted history of these palm-kissed islands than Jim Cumbes, than whom nobody kept it tighter at New Road (except possibly Cedric Boyns)?

And after his performance at the Pegasus Hotel on Monday evening Mike Denness – cheeky, but never blue – shot up no less than 20 places in the Coopers & Lybrand After-Dinner Speech Rankings. Clearly there was no one better equipped than 'Denness the Menness' to be called on for an impromptu pre-lunch speech on Thursday morning, when the game was called off.

Which is something that would never have happened in my day. What a load of Moaning Minnies! I suppose the writing was on the wall earlier this week, when the A team got on the blower to Lord's at the first whiff of a suicide bombing at the Temple of the Tooth in Sri Lanka (or Sri Lon as it used to be called in Keith Fletcher's time).

I have to say I was on the side of the Hon. Tim Lamb for once, when he said the young gentlemen were being rather wet. That is Pod's philosophy too, and it went down very well with the two dozen less-than-gruntled Ian Treen customers in the George Headley Stand on Thursday. So did my suggestion that Athers should have declared at 17 for 3 – which after all represents a fairly useful effort for an England side in the Caribbean – stuck the oppo in and let Caddy off the leash.

The other mistake, which could have been fatal had the game gone into a second hour, was to put Alec Stewart down to keep wicket. The obvious candidate and an ideal man for the job is surely Angus Fraser. He's slowed down in the last couple of years, has Gus – so he could easily deliver the ball and still have plenty of time to get down the other end, slip the gloves on and catch it.

Gus would also provide useful cover for Jack Russell, who is up every night with the squits as he tries to work out how long to boil his flying fish to the precise half-minute. Either way, Stewie is free to concentrate on his batting, which is what he is there for at the end of the day, or the end of the first drinks break as I suppose we should say now.

But the greatest disappointment of the first Test for me was that we had no chance to have a look at the new Windies pace ace Nixon McLean. All we know about him is that he and the rest of his family are named after American presidents. I hear that he may well be dropped in Trinidad in favour of his younger brother Clinton – by all accounts a useful performer with a deadly full-length delivery, which suddenly veers off at 45 degrees at the top of its trajectory.

2 February 1998

Good-natured rivalry leads
to an expedition.

It's starting to get a tiny bit much. After last week's less-than-Happy Hour on the corrugated-iron roof of Sabina Park, the tour was thrown into complete chaos. The lads' carefully-prepared relaxation schedule has been blown out of the water. No sooner do we land in Trinidad than we're plunged into hastily rearranged back-to-back scuba-diving trips and cocktail parties at the Governor's mansion, not to mention the bloody carnival. I'm sure our hosts mean well, but there is a limit. Frankly we've all had enough and just want to come home.

On top of everything else we're still having to cope with the wandering hordes of what Nass Hussain (the wag of the party) calls SBOFGOOPs – Sad Bastards Over Five Grand Out Of Pocket – wanting us to chat with them in the hotel and sign their souvenir First Test programmes. I ask you.

The facilities remain a joke, especially with regard to the beach cricket. The other evening we had to abandon a promising session at Chickie's Conch Shell Bar-B-Q because the corrugated-iron roof was far too flat. You could have staged a Test match on it, and the lads quite justifiably rebelled.

As for the actual playing surface: you try bowling 30 overs off the reel through three feet of soft sand, with the ever-present possibility of picking up a jellyfish niggle. It nearly did for poor old Gus. Chris Silverwood can count himself lucky nobody told him the venue.

And that brings me on to the Mark Ramprakash situation, which has been building up for some time. It's always a shame when a tour party splits into factions, but since day one there's been a widening gap between the sit-by-the-pool tendency and the fitness freaks who play for Surrey and want to go off para-gliding.

Ramps can't get into either camp. Finding something to do when you aren't picked can be a problem, but he didn't sulk or superglue the last dozen pages of the skipper's thriller together – an episode which marked the beginning of the end for Dave Pod-more and Derbyshire. No, Ramps decided to go off on his own, exploring the hinterland. And fair play to him, he's racked up 29 species of Caribbean flora and fauna in no time at all. Trouble is, being Ramps, he just can't seem to get into those elusive 30s.

We didn't think too much about it when he didn't appear at breakfast for three days, assuming he was on the scent of the rare Scarlet Ibis, not to be confused with its ubiquitous brother, the Red Striped Ibis. But then on the first morning of the current Test, Bob Bennett gets a call from the Middlesex captain on his mobile. Apparently he's out there in the hinterland, stuck up Mount Lara (formerly Mount Learie). Poor old Ramps. Not only have the wheels come off his tour, they've now come off his mini-moke.

Never one to miss an opportunity, Adam Hollioake quickly organised a crack rescue team from his Surrey colleagues and before you could say 'one-day wonders' they were off across the savannah, pausing only for Stewie to gather up his brushes and easel. He takes his duties as cover for Jack Russell very seriously indeed.

Half an hour before Athers is due to go out for the toss, who should happen to stroll into the ground, looking like butter wouldn't melt, but Messrs Ramprakash, Croft, Silverwood and Cowan, all kitted out and sun-block applied. Nice try, guys, but you hadn't reckoned on the legendary athleticism of the Surrey Lions, who soon realised they'd been had. They covered the 14-mile jog from Mount Lara in a little under the hour, and at that moment the four of them were already in the pavilion, also kitted out and indulging in a little arm-wrestling to blow the cobwebs away.

To rub further salt in, Stewie even had time to execute a neat sketch of the Scarlet Ibis – professional as you like and not a feather out of place. His timely 50 in the match, not to mention Thorpey's commanding 8 and Hollioake's fighting 2 (complete with moral victory) should ensure Ramps is kept busy carrying the rum punch for a long time to come.

Finally, a note for the *Guardian*'s Corrections and Clarifications Department. In my column last week I discussed the ramifications of the Sabina Park affair and possible courses of action to be taken against the Jamaican cricket authorities. I now realise that the word 'disembowelling' has only one W. Apologies all round.

A board game sorts out the men from the boys.

Eight weeks into the tour and it's still too close to call. After the heart-stopping, nerve-jangling, two-Test cauldron of Trinidad nobody can be said to have the advantage. What a game! If you've never played Balderdash it's probably very difficult to understand how physically and mentally draining it can be.

At least if you're out on the field playing cricket it takes your mind off it for a few hours every day. But for the rest of the squad and those of us in the back-up team the pressure can be unbearable. Especially now we're in Guyana, which is not an island but in South America, apparently. We'd all been looking forward to this leg of the tour because Guyana is famous for its rain and for riots that can usually guarantee 10 days solid in the hotel.

There's the odd bit of scenery to be checked out, but quite frankly once you've seen one 2000-foot waterfall in a total eclipse you've seen them all. Most of the lads just wanted to get back to Crofty's room at the Pegasus and get on with the game.

As every cricket-history buff knows, an England overseas party's board game of choice has traditionally been Monopoly. That was until a couple of tours back, when Mike Gatting ate the top hat, the Scottie dog and the boot. Fair play to Gatt, it had been a curtailed lunch interval, and mostly fruit at that. The poor guy was starving. For a while we muddled along with the contents of Steve Bucknor's pockets, but had to give them back when the match referee decided that 265 balls was enough for one over.

Balderdash, which has been introduced as part of Lord MacLaurin's sweeping changes, is a game for four or more cricketers and is a bit like Call My Bluff except without women, obviously. (But for how much longer that will be, your guess is as good as mine, my friend.) Basically one team defines what a word means but not always correctly and the other team has to guess which is the right one (definition, that is). Can get a bit complicated, so it helps to have one of the university eggheads like Bungalow Bollocks or Burger Arse on your side.

Take a word like Cork, for instance. The dictionary will tell you that it's something D. I. Gower Esq. sticks in his bottle of vino posho to stop his room-mate having a slash in it in the middle of the night. But Pod walked away with the points for coming up with: 'A prima donna who thinks that just because he takes one Test hat-trick and wears a lot of face-paint he can go running to the media every time he doesn't get the nod.'

Memo to young Master Dominic: if you're not happy with your situation, I suggest that instead of moaning and groaning you knuckle down and find another county to play for. Parting company with Derbyshire is never a bad career move; indeed I've done it myself three times, if memory serves. Better to follow the example of Devon Malcolm, now happily ensconced at Northants – although Dev being Dev he'd originally aimed for Somerset.

Anyway, as I say, Pod was on a bit of a roll and looking good Balderdashwise. So you can imagine my degree of guttedness when the team's set went missing this week. Stuck in Guyana without a board game; no wonder those Jim Jones guys committed mass suicide. Needless to say, a huge search was instigated involving all the usual suspects, starting with the baggage handlers at the airport who've so far been responsible for everything else that's gone seriously astray (or 'Headley-ed' as they say in Balderdash).

Athers' girlfriend's dad even made space in the local rag to report the loss. A hunt among the wreckage outside Tuffers' hotel-room window produced nothing more than a mini-bar, a trouser press and two TV sets, although you had to admire the characteristic way he'd landed everything on exactly the same spot. Finally we had no alternative but to call in Steve Bull, the team psychotherapist, who painstakingly built up a character profile of the most likely culprit.

Not much gets past Steve in the way of character flaws (or 'Caddicks' as they say in Balderdash) and no sooner has Steve started his one-on-one investigations than Adam Hollioake holds up his hand and confesses he's had the set in his room all along. It seems Oakey had been having a bit of a practice on his own, the long-term aim being to replace Athers as gamesmeister and keeper of the boxes – proving in no uncertain terms that if you're good enough at Balderdash then you're old enough.

Game on again.

A question of jewellery.

It's been a bad week. Jacqui arrived in Barbados with the other wives and fiancees on the Crumpet Plane with some shocking news. She'd taken my dogs on the Countryside March last Sunday and they'd all come back with hard pad. An Alsatian's paws are more sensitive than people realise. Just wait till our wonderful Government gets my vet's bills.

This is after Jacqui has been delayed for several hours at the airport. She was already in a right mood about the other week, when I described how she was coming over on the Crumpet Plane, or Totty Tristar. This was because I spelt her name with two k's by mistake, getting her mixed up with the second Mrs Podmore. Oops. If I'd had my sponsored car here with me I'd have been sleeping in it, I can tell you.

Anyway, Jacqui did quite a bit of modelling a few years back before she got the Viking Direct catalogue gig, and the customs officers recognised her from a batch of Dutch magazines which had been impounded for some reason. What with one thing and another it took her a good couple of hours to get through passport control here.

So by the time we got to the official welcoming party at Government House it's hardly surprising Jacqui was in dire need of a rum punch or two. But to say she was drunk, as the gentlemen of certain tabloid media have alleged, is totally libellous. She'd accidentally got her ankle chain caught in the back of one of her stilettoes – a networking incident that could happen to any fashion-conscious young woman.

But there has been one bright spot this week. The Guyana Test finished a day early, which allowed the lads to spend some quality time getting their various acts together. Tuffers chose to work hard on his fielding, which – as every commentator will tell you – he's been doing for some years. All he needs to do now is work a bit on his bowling.

Our entire bowling attack is struggling with the same problem at the moment, a typically English one. The team just isn't wearing enough jewellery, whereas with Ambrose and Walsh the Windies have two bowlers who have both broken Fred Trueman's record of 300 ounces of gold worn at a Test match.

Of course you're going to overstep and get no-balled if you arrive at the crease without proper ballast round your neck. The Second Test was decided by sheer weight of necklaces, and the current one will be too. You mark my words.

The captain resigns after England lose the series.

At long last Dave Podmore is free to speak his mind about the former England skipper. Of course I was never anything less than 350% loyal to Mike Atherton as long as he was in the driving seat, but now he's gone I have to say – along with many of my colleagues in the media – that he was a right stuck-up little clever clogs who hadn't a clue how to approach the art of captaincy. It's no secret that by the time he resigned most of the dressing-room was behind him only 100%. And you can't go on like that.

Having said that, the guy made a very promising start to his time in charge. When my old dad (Dave Podmore) kicked the bucket back in 1994, his last wish was to have his ashes scattered at Lord's. It was a very special and moving moment during the England v South Africa Test when Athers bent down, picked Dad up and put him in his pocket.

Next thing I know he's rubbed quite a bit of Dad onto the ball and chucked it to Goughie, who in turn dropped one short and wallop – Dad's being clattered through the covers for four by Kepler Wessels to take him into double figures. I think it's what Dad would have wanted.

Unfortunately that bit of ball-tampering was as good as it got from Athers, tactically speaking. It wasn't long before the less acceptable, Oxbridge University side of his character started coming to the fore. We should have seen the danger signs the previous summer in Birmingham when he made the lads go and see *The Piano* instead of *Lethal Weapon 3*, which was playing next door in the multiplex. Fortunately the sound came through the wall and drowned out a fair bit of the arty-farty dialogue.

From then on there was an ever-widening gulf between the skipper and the rest of the team. It's hard to relate to someone who goes out with the same bird for four years and spends the rest of his leisure time with his nose in a 1000-page hardback novel. A Suitable Boy? Pod begs to differ.

But what really worries me about Atherton is that he's reached the ripe old age of 30 without acquiring any of the necessary PR skills to carry him through his post-captaincy years. Anyone who'd seen his pathetic attempts at networking, as I did during the Kwik-Fit Fitters' function at Wolverhampton all-weather races, would know what I mean. If he can't hack it there he's hardly likely to get very far in the much more demanding and occasionally brutal world of pantomime.

He's got to be prepared to go back to basics and learn his trade.

A tour remembered.

First of all, let me say from the outset that, contrary to what you may have seen in the media, Dave Podmore has not been sent home. In no way have my bits-and-pieces skills been deemed inferior to those of Old Etonian Matthew Fleming or Mark Ealham or any of the other guys with famous dads.

The reasons were entirely personal. I made it clear to the selectors at the start of the tour that I would have to come back early and thus be unavailable for most of the one-dayers. The date for my appearance at Hinckley Magistrates Court was set months ago.

If they will insist on putting school playing fields in full view of a guy's picture window, what do they expect? Ultimately it's my word against that of three dozen schoolgirls. I have every confidence of getting a result, especially in the light of the recent verdict across the pond in Little Rock. I reckon I'm looking at 100 hours' community service tops, and the way I see it, digging a few pensioners' allotments will get me fit and cherry-ripe to join my new county colleagues for their pre-season bonding weekend in Portugal.

Talking of cricket, I was very disappointed to have to leave the tour just when the lads were finding some extra gears, to spectacular effect. Last Wednesday was quite simply the best April Fool's Day I've had the privilege of being involved with in all my 23 years in the first-class game. The fax congratulating Stewie on getting in the frame to be the new Lord Mayor of London was inspired, second only to whoever it was slipped a canister of anthrax into Thorpey's hand-luggage. And Athers eventually saw the funny side of the electric fire being thrown into his jacuzzi (Nick Knight – pinpoint accuracy as usual).

Of course there was the odd damp squib. I'm happy to report that I saw the wind-up about D. V. Podmore being one of *Wisden*'s Five Cricketers of the Year coming a mile off, as I did when Brian Bolus first tried it out on me in 1973.

So, as I say, it was a bit of a wrench saying Goodnight Vienna to the Caribbean. But luckily I had company on the way home. If you can call it company; instead of sitting next to me, Thorpey was given a row of seats across the aisle to himself on account of his back condition. Fair play, he'd had two very bad spasms, one in Antigua which led to Nasser Hussain being run out and the Sixth Test (and the series) being lost, and another spasm in Bridgetown resulting in Knighty getting sawn off in the 120s, nearly costing us that match as well.

I reminded Thorpey of this over a medicinal miniature, and we fell to reminiscing about other highlights of the tour. Such as the moment during the Trinidad carnival when there was a request for Crofty to turn down his Discman from the Amoco Renegades steel band, who couldn't hear themselves think for Tom Jones.

Then there was the equally ear-splitting noise of Curtly Ambrose's mum, ringing a bell every time her boy took a wicket. Not to be outdone, Andy Caddick's mum out in New Zealand sounded the horn on her Triumph Herald every time the press said he had a flawed character. Nobody got much sleep in Christchurch over the last few months, I can tell you.

Golden memories. And now here I am back home, eating a kebab that I've had to microwave myself. Jacqui's got a strop on because one of the dogs has bitten a baby. Perhaps that's because someone hasn't been feeding it properly. On top of everything, I've discovered I've missed the car registration changeover date. Every other bugger and his wife it seems is driving round in an 'R' reg while Pod is still stuck with a 'P' – for plonker.

But that's cricket. At least I've come back with a fistful of tickets for Jamaica's World Cup matches. If I can't sell them down at the golf club tomorrow I've no right to call myself a professional sportsman.

8

The New
Ian Botham Arena

Whenever the national side finds itself up an excrement inlet minus rowing implements – about 10 times a year on average, not including ODIs – the call goes out for a New Ian Botham. It's a bit like the old chestnut about shouting down a pit and up would come an England fast bowler. What finally knocked that scenario on the head was when the only pits left in the country were in Wales, and someone shouted down one and up came Crofty.

I'm afraid this New Ian Botham (or NIB) palaver just leaves Pod on the comatose side of tired. How many NIBs have we seen in recent years, not including myself about which more later? It happened to Ian Greig, David Capel, Chris Cowdrey, Chris Lewis, Craig White, Ronnie Irani – all new Bothams. Even Mark Alleyne. Actually I think he was the new Derek Pringle, but you get the point I'm making about the burden of expectancy.

The truth is that none of these guys, excellent companions

who you can have a drink and light a fart with though they may be, could even begin to approach the foothills of Mount Beefy with his impeccable Renaissance Man credentials. So this section is intended as a friendly warning to the current crop of would-be NIBs: to show them just how far they've got to go, and I don't mean over the Alps with an elephant.

It wouldn't be right not to finish without my tribute to the New Ian Botham of his generation, a certain Australian gentleman called D. G. Bradman Esq., as adept apparently at tinkling the ivories as he was at smacking a Bodyline bowler back over his head. Sadly the Don died soon after receiving my open letter so he couldn't e-mail back, which was sad but there we are.

An open letter to Andrew Flintoff.

Dear Andrew,

I know how you must have felt when you saw your name on Ceefax as one of the England squad on Sunday morning. Actually I know the exact feeling, because it happened to me last year when Spamhead and Co. did a wind-up, bunging some bloke at the BBC to flash my name up for a couple of minutes and then ringing me with the great news. Tossers.

But I hope you'll allow yourself to be vouchsafed some words of advice from somebody who's been knocking around long enough to learn a thing or two about the game of cricket. In fact it's fair to say that Pod's been there, done that and got through a good few t-shirts. Also pants and socks.

Over the next few weeks, Andrew, you're going to read a lot of eyewash about you being the next Ian Botham. Sure, you could go that route, steaming in at a rate of knots, knocking a lot of guys' poles out and scoring Test hundreds in better than even time. But the danger is that – like Beefy – you'll find yourself burned out by the time you're 37.

Alternatively you could do yourself a favour, be a bit clever and pace yourself. It hasn't worked out too badly for Dave Podmore: six benefits and another one on the way, a Shogun in the car-port and a tidy couple of hundred grand ticking over nicely in the Halifax. Not bad for someone who at the age of 45 is

supposedly 'over the hill, overweight and overpaid', according to the kind gentleman who freephoned in to Radio Trent.

Andrew, the reason I'm telling you this is because I was once a jug-eared teenager in your position. I was in my second season for Derbyshire, I'd had a winter in South Africa when it really was South Africa, I was being sponsored for a tin of dog-food every time I took a wicket. I knew it all, didn't I? The young Pod

144

was a cocky so-and-so heading for a right royal comeuppance – which I don't want to happen to you.

Sharing a room with Ted Crapp on the South-Western tour was the greatest slice of luck, not to mention privilege, a 17-year-old could wish for. You probably won't have heard of the legendary Ted, Andrew. He's not in the record books and you won't see him on the *Golden Greats Of The Seventies* video alongside the likes of Geoff Miller and Bev Congdon. But I've never seen anyone do more with the ball than Ted could.

They talk about players with flair – well, Ted had flares, 17-inch ones they were. He could walk around with a pump-action screwdriver strapped to each calf and the umpires never noticed a thing.

I idolised Ted. I remember once even running myself out to ensure an early finish in the John Player, because I knew Ted wanted to get home in time for the Black and White Minstrels. He never thanked me for it, of course, just nicked my towel and told me to get him a Mackeson. That was Ted all over.

The fact that youngsters no longer get the chance to share a room and sometimes a bed with a senior pro is a great loss to the game, and to my mind one of the things that's landed us in our current doldrum. In an ideal world I'd have been able to room with you too, Andrew, but as it is you'll have to make do with these words to the wise.

What you can do for yourself right now, if you want to emulate His Royal Beefiness, is forget about winning those Ashes single-handed this winter. Instead, get your name on a pantomime poster, appear on a light-hearted sports quiz and find a disease that nobody's done an elephant walk in aid of. Oh, and sort out your views on capital punishment, ready for that question-and-answer roadshow. If you're sadistic enough, you're old enough, I say.

You do need to work on the fitness aspect of your game. Whenever possible pick up a niggle – groin, fingers, curvature of the spine – and declare yourself unavailable. Because if you're not careful you'll keep being picked to play for England. And that's the last thing a promising young player needs.

Cheers,

A word of warning to Alex Tudor.

It being the silly season part of the season, there's been a lot of trumpeting of Alex Tudor as the next New Ian Botham. I remember when I was similarly trumpeted. One week Dave Podmore was the saviour of the nation. The next he was public enemy number one. So my advice to the boy Alex is: never forget that the trumpet can be a two-edged sword.

Take nothing away from the 20-whatever-year-old. He's done well to get into the history books as a nightwatchman, alongside the likes of Harold Larwood, Eddie Hemmings and myself. But as this cautionary little tale shows, he'd be advised not to get big-headed and go swanning around the circuit giving it large and bringing his agent in the dressing-room, because he's only produced the goods once and he hasn't convinced Pod yet so he just wants to watch it.

It still gives me a buzz when people tell me they remember my own heroics in the emergency batter's role at Edgbaston in '89. Curtis, Moxon, Maynard and Chris Cowdrey had all been unlucky enough to get straight ones, and with the board reading 1 for 4 D. V. Podmore walked out to face Marshall and Ambrose. Thirty-seven overs and three changes of trousers later I was still there.

Obviously if you look at the bare statistics in *Old Wisden's Almanack*, you'd have to say that, on paper, 0 looks like a lowish score. But it doesn't take into account the 23 leg byes (eight off my helmet and 15 off my arse) that helped us to reach the relative respectability of 61 all out.

I knew that if I could just jump away towards square leg whenever I got a short one and have a wild swing at anything that was pitched up and in my slot then eventually the runs would start to flow. And flow they did, albeit in extras. You'd have to say that, in real terms, I was top scorer, with only Hicky's 12 and Ramps's three-hour 2 not out giving me any meaningful support.

In the end I was very unlucky to get out. To be bowled off your shoulder isn't something anyone enjoys but it happens to even the greatest players. And if I'd managed to crouch down even lower it would have definitely been a wide, because as the replay showed it was a good five feet outside leg peg.

Quite simply, that was one of the toughest charity matches I've ever played in. If Marshall and Ambrose had been bowling right-arm over instead of left-arm under it would have been total carnage out there. And if it had been Malcolm instead of Gordon Marshall and Curtly rather than Graham Ambrose of Euro Kitchens we'd really have been in the poo big-style.

I emerged with most of the honours for gutsing it out and what with the merry mayhem I orchestrated in the hotel afterwards the Sunday papers made a big thing of it. Sure, a couple of king-size beds got broken, a mini-bar or three took a pounding and eight hospitality lasses had a tale to tell. But for the media to go trumpeting Dave Podmore as the Next Ian Botham was just putting too much pressure on me. No way could I be expected to produce that level of horseplay day in day out.

The very next weekend, I'm in another hotel corridor stark

naked and caught short into the bargain (as is so often the case in these stories). As luck would have it, Brian Johnston had left a pair of his famous two-tone shoes outside his door ready to be cleaned. I followed my instincts and the rest is tabloid history: 'Going to the Johnners', etc.

But suddenly you find that far from being the new Botham you now represent the ugly face of cricket. And for what? A simple error of judgment. But that's the wonderful country we live in: they build a guy up simply in order to knock him down again.

So you see Alex Tudor, my young friend, they can do to you what they did to Pod. And a final word on that so-called 99 not out: I've heard a whisper that some of the posher press-box boys bunged the Kiwi trundlers to go easy on the nightwatchman just so they could run a very clever 'Tudors and Stewarts' headline.

Two of a Future *Wisden* 'Five'?

There's a bush telegraph in the game they call cricket, and when news filtered through from the last A tour of Bangladesh about young Banger Trescothick we all got very excited – the Powers That Be had found what they'd been looking for since the 1980s. Anyone who saw Marcus's Scary Spice impersonation knew instantly that England had unearthed a Christmas party performer to rank with the greats like Chris Tavare and Neil Foster. The young left-hander kept his wig on for several hours in blistering heat, which shows he's got the appetite for the job, and Duncan Fletcher's been banging his drum ever since.

Of course he's not quite the newcomer the media have portrayed. Banger's been involved with the England set-up from Under-14 level (where he showed amazing maturity as Tina Turner in a Saturday night get-together at Lilleshall). He had a couple of years in the doldrums recently and perhaps put on a little bit too much weight, and it's only natural that if a guy can't get into his frock, well, it's going to affect his form out in the middle.

But now he's back to his best and as far as Pod's concerned the lad's ready to take the big step up. If the selectors are searching for someone to provide the very best in interval entertainment for the ODIs they need look no further than the Keynsham southpaw. Obviously I'm disappointed at the phasing-out of my own pilot scheme – Two Giant Transparent Balls Rolling Slowly

Across The Outfield™ – especially as I'm not going to be able to get them in the garage even when they're deflated. But I accept that the game's got to go forward, and if we didn't move with the times we'd all be living in caves with animal skins on our backs (a concept which we also experimented with once at Headingley).

Talk of youth and Yorkshire brings me to their own fresh-faced white rosebud Steve Kirby. I've been getting a lot of credit for the work I've done with the fiery redhead on his in-yer-face attitude. But in all honesty it was just fine tuning. He worked as a carpet fitter for four years after Leicester sacked him, so by the time he came to me there wasn't a lot I could teach him about following up each delivery with a torrent of abuse. Although it did take a while to get his run-up right, as he still had a tendency to approach the crease in a white van hooting and flashing his lights.

Pod's Footnote

I'm pleased to say the Powers That Be have had second thoughts and restored the Transparent Balls to their rightful place at the centrepiece of every cricket meal break.

An Open Letter to a Legend.

Dear Sir 'The Don' Bradman,

Pod's had a bit of time on his hands this weekend (Gloucestershire hired me as a consultant to spot any loopholes, in case they didn't win the NatWest Final) so I thought I'd sit down and send you best wishes on your 90-oddth birthday which they tell me was on Sunday, or tomorrow our time.

The name Podmore might not be as famous as Bradman down under, but we've both been pros long enough to have gained the reputation as respected observers of the game. Our cricketing skills were honed at an early age – yours by hitting a golf ball against a water tank with a stump. Not being born with a silver spoon the young Pod had to make do with a stick and some frogs down by the Erewash Canal – four if they landed in the water, six if they made it to the opposite bank (and five if they came apart in mid-air).

The similarities don't end there. Take our international careers. Everybody knows that you fell just four runs short of having a Test average of 100. And by weird coincidence that's exactly my Test average – 4, a boundary scored off a thick edge in my solitary England appearance against Sri Lanka.

There's been some carping over the years that I only got those runs because the slip cordon was distracted by a stand being burnt down by Tamils. But it's there in the record books for all to see, and they can't take it away from me. Anyway, it's better than getting a duck in your last Test innings, isn't it, sport?

Over the years our families have both had to play second fiddle to our careers, and this has led to understandable friction. I gather your son even changed his name because he was having trouble living in the shadow of greatness. We've all been there, having to deal with a young 'un who doesn't always shape up to his dad's expectations, be it Len and Richard Hutton, Colin and Chris Cowdrey, or Harry and Matthew Corbett.

Dave Podmore Junior is often threatening to change his name – most recently after my appearance on *A Question of Sport*. If it ever comes Australia's way on BBC Choice, I'd choose not to watch that particular episode, mate. I won't go into the gory details, but it was then that the Powers That Be decided to introduce routine drug tests after every recording.

I was told that your lad was now known as Dannii Minogue and I nearly fell for it, but it was only Clive Rice with his goonish sense of humour trying to inject some cheer into the Notts dressing-room. In any case, I hear you've just got compensation big-style with a whole street in Adelaide being named in your honour.

I can't yet aspire to those heights of fame, but let me draw your attention to the Pod Bap ('Everything under the sun in a bun') which made its triumphant debut at the Trent Bridge Inn this season during the floodlit National League match against Warwickshire. It's a sort of enhanced BLT, with extra layers of S, E, CB and B sauce, and will keep you going for a couple of days, about the length of the average Test match over here. Just the thing for sticking into your tucker bag and taking on that hike into the outback.

And the problem with having a place named after you is that you can't always control the sort of people who live and work there. Look at all those Nelson Mandela Houses, and the trouble they've caused. Though I have to say I think you've lost the plot a bit, trying to stop that sex shop in Adelaide calling itself 'Erotica on Bradman'. You've got to look after your interests off the park in this game, The Don, and my advice would be to let the guys go ahead with their enterprise – just make sure you get a complimentary consignment of the merchandise.

You wouldn't have to use it yourself, but it's handy to have around in case the barbie goes flat and you're stuck for entertainment ideas. Or Pod would be happy to take said wares off your hands – I'd even pay the postage. Better still, bring it over here yourself and apply to be Notts' overseas player next season. I know they're starting to look around for somebody and that ton of experience you've got under your belt might be just the thing to shore up the middle order.

Sorry, got to sign off now – there's just been a stumping decision against the Glos boys, and they're talking about taking it to the European Court of Human Rights.

Many happy returns and all the breast,

9

The Innovative
Solutions Arena

Not for nothing does Pod have the reputation on the circuit of being one of the game's most forward-looking thinkers. The way I see it, we've all got the opportunity to shape the kind of cricketing world order we want – to leave something not only for our children, but for our fiancees' children too.

I was the first person to realise the full potential of the stump microphone, and it came about during my last spell at Notts. It didn't really work out for me at Trent Bridge, any more than it did in 1994 or 1983 or 1975 come to think of it. But the little time I spent out in the middle was highly productive. By fielding close to the wicket and speaking directly and clearly into the stump microphone I managed to advertise and sell a couple of old bats, a washing machine and that bloody computer I bought for the kids off Mr Spock.

Since then the stump mike, it's fair to say, has revolutionised the game for the senior pro in search of pastures new. As a cheap and efficient means of announcing your availability for next season it's hard to beat. In fact, between overs you sometimes have to fight to get near it. But as I say, healthy competition can only be good for cricket in the long term.

It's in the nature of the job that we spend a lot of time watching daytime television in the dressing room, which explains the above-average occurrence of cricketers' kids called Kilroy and Oprah. And daytime TV is very much the focus of Pod's future plans. I've got high hopes that the Channel 5 bosses will give the green light nod to 'Celebrity Roadkill', where people with busy travelling schedules get points and possibly prizes for the endangered species they've accidentally wiped out. BBC1 have expressed an interest but I don't want to see the idea dragged downmarket and turned into just another cheap run-over show.

Here are some of Pod's other ideas for making the world of cricket a more lucrative place.

Far-reaching plans for an Academy of Cricketing Excellence.

We've got to do something to restore our national pride. And fast, otherwise if things carry on the way they are we might just as well go the British Airways tail-fin route, i.e. turn the whole shooting match over to a bunch of foreigners with paint guns.

So let me put it on record that the fightback starts here. The Dave Podmore Academy of Cricketing Excellence will be opening its doors for business as soon as we get the nod from the Lottery boys. The key to sporting success in the global arena can be summed up in one word: preparation, preparation, preparation. It's been the same down the centuries. What stuffed Napoleon on the playing fields of Eton wasn't that it was an away fixture. Our lads had done their homework, it was as simple as that.

And that's what we're going to do at the Bits and Pieces Academy. Every aspect of our players' games will be exhaustively analysed and corrected. Mister Sloppiness will be given his marching orders. I've lost count of the number of times this season I've seen a young player gobbing out his chewing gum after he's been dismissed. He opens the face of his bat, takes a big swing, far too much bottom hand, result? The lad's missed his gum by a country mile. This sends out entirely the wrong signals to the opposition, and just like an inaccurate nasal clearance, it hands them the psychological advantage on a plate.

Getting the Bombay mix out of your jock-strap, avoiding that slap in the face from an outraged hospitality lass – these are just some of the problems we'll be ironing out. We'll be turning our students into world-beaters, but more important than that, we'll be turning them into world-beaters with properly-structured, long-term clothing endorsement deals. Never again will a youngster suffer the embarrassment of turning up for a post-match interview not knowing if he's supposed to wear the sweater with the little thistle on or the one with the bear in pads.

We've been lucky enough to enlist the services of Chris Broad as special consultant. Chris isn't appearing on TV quite as much as he was hoping to now Boycs is back in the frame, but the viewers' loss is the future of the game's gain. He's also consented to be our Slacks and Slip-On Shoes Czar.

No doubt the Bits and Pieces Academy will attract its fair share of doubters, but Pod is confident that once these seemingly trivial details are taken care of off the field, then as sure as night follows day/night the results will start to go our way on the park.

Once we're up and running with the Lottery loot, we'll need someone to come in for the odd kazillion or two. Let's face it, Nike backed a loser with Brazil on the footy field, so I'm giving them a chance early doors to be on the winning side for once.

The Academy's motto? *Just Do It* (yourself justice, that is).

Arguments in support
of the Third Way.

In the light of one or two recent controversial decisions both here in the West Indies and on the sub-continent, no one can be in any doubt about what the hardest job in world cricket is. And that's getting the nod to be the third umpire as opposed to having to stand out in the middle the whole day, being abused by all and sundry.

Dave Podmore's views on umpire protection are well known and I understand that my recommendations for issuing all match officials with semi-automatic firearms are being looked on favourably at Lord's – although I realise they've got a lot on their plates at the moment dealing with the whingeing women from the Pro-Life brigade. I dunno, one minute they're demanding to be admitted to the Long Room, the next they want to stay at home and have babies. I wish they'd make up their minds.

Umpires place themselves at great personal peril and, the way I see it, a discreet bulge in the jacket and a slight risk of accidents is a small price to pay for peace of mind. And anyway most first-class grounds boast a St John's ambulance with two blokes who never have anything else to deal with apart from the odd Thermos injury.

Unfortunately, violence and intimidation are increasingly a feature of the international game. It's sad when someone as respected as Wasim Akram says he's afraid to go out of the house

without a gun, although to be fair everyone else who lives in Manchester says the same thing.

Then there were the two disgraceful incidents during the recent Barbados Test: one when Mister Lara viciously criticised Stewie for claiming a catch off a bump ball, the other when Philo Wallace and Clayton Lambert cynically persisted in hitting Angus Fraser all round the park in flagrant contravention of the rules of sportsmanship.

All of which carryings-on are very good reasons for an umpire to get himself out of the firing line and up behind the protective glass of that little box at the top of the pavilion, feet up in front of the telly with a complimentary Cable and Wireless picnic hamper by your side – what could be better?

Third umpiring has to be the top job in the international sports arena right now. By and large you're sat there relaxing in comfort like a Roman emperor in olden times, except they didn't have a channel changer in those days obviously. Nigel Plews told me that the last time he was third-umpiring, out in New Zealand, he managed to catch several editions of *One Man And His Dog* which he'd missed in the '70s – and what's more they were as good as ever.

And if you're busy surfing some of the more exotic satellite channels being beamed in from Malaysia and happen to miss the replay of a disputed run-out, or if for any other reason you find yourself making a piss-hole decision, not to worry. There's always a match referee who'll back you up and tell the press it was just one of those unfortunate things that sometimes happen in this great game of cricket.

Towards a more democratic way of being dismissed.

'No one goes into a match deliberately intending to drop a catch.' That's what Shane Warne said when the media asked him about the 18-odd let-offs his boys have had in the last two Tests. It's a typically unsophisticated Aussie way of looking at it, but there is a grain of truth in Warnie's words. Just when you think you're on fire in the field, that's when you find yourself fetching it off the floor and chewing your gum extra hard while everyone around you shouts, 'Bad luck Poddy, back on the button boys, it's coming.'

On the other hand if someone has bunged you a few thousand rand, a leather jacket or whatever to deck one then sod's law guarantees that when a half chance comes along you'll pouch it lemon-bleeding-squeezy. It's the way life is, i.e. unfair.

Catching is one of the most humiliating aspects of the game of cricket, which is why I personally would like to see it done away with as a form of dismissal. Nobody wants to see their hero running round in circles under a skyer before falling into a heap. These days I always field close to the bat, that way you've shelled it and got it back to the bowler before anyone in the Members' has spotted there was a chance. Even so you're always struggling to hold on to your dignity.

Now you might say that removing the catch from your wicket-taking options would make beating the Aussies an even bigger ask but the point is we wouldn't look so crap. In any case, the few dollies we do manage to cling on to are mostly off no-balls, so to my way of thinking catches are just another way of slowing the game down and alienating the youngsters, especially when you've then got to hang around for Steve Bucknor to get his finger into gear. Pod advocates a more proactive, new millennium way of being given out.

It operates on the *Big Brother* principle whereby the third umpire would invite viewers to ring in and vote on whether or not a batsman should stay at the crease. So his fate wouldn't just be decided by his batting skills, it'd include other stuff like being big-headed, having weird eyes or a bad haircut etc.

Trying to reach your century by chipping it over Stewie's head for six? Thirty-nine votes says you're too cocky by half, Mister Gilchrist – on your way back to the pavilion mate. You see, if you've got the technology it makes no sense not to use it. Calls would be charged at premium rate but everyone who participates would also be entered in a prize draw which could win them an unforgettable day at Trent Bridge, as England's third seamer.

Penalties for over-confidence could well be the chink in the Aussie armour. Dave Podmore would give them all red cards for the way they hold the ball up to the crowd every time one of them takes a five-for. I know they're a young country and bursting with pride at being allowed to trade punches with more ancient civilisations, but like all stroppy kids they've got to learn when to button it.

So assuming the Powers That Be adopt Pod's proposals, all we'll need to get those Ashes back on the mantelpiece is a bit more self-belief. A lot of media wiseacres have tried to analyse why we're so lacking in that department. Mike Brearley probably reckons it's to do with all the lads wanting to get off with their mums or something. But I think it goes a lot deeper than that.

Surely money is at the root of this particular evil. Look at the country's top executives. Apparently the guys who run the railways, Marks and Spencer's and the like each take home on average around half a million quid. Fine. Got no problem with that. It's a stressful occupation getting the trains to run on tracks and coming up with different shades of beige for the trousers. But a cricketer's job is stressful too.

Look at Ian Woosnam. He walks onto the golf course with too many clubs in his bag. It costs him 200 grand but he still ends up with a six-figure wage packet. Dave Podmore steps onto the park with four bats, all with separate sponsors' logos, and he can barely feed his dogs on the proceeds.

There's your answer to our sporting underachievement. Change the rules, pay us more money and let's concentrate on those traditional English strengths like reality TV.

New Zealand win the Second Test by nine wickets.

Like it says in the song, things can hardly get any better. Anyone who was at Lord's last week couldn't not be impressed by the state-of-the-art debenture seating areas packed to bursting or the queues for the Le Burger d'Or bar snaking through the indoor school.

Nobody who joined me amid the bustling surroundings of the Croissant Village could seriously suggest that there's too much wrong with English cricket. Channel 4's exciting new technology was bringing in a whole new audience analysing the sound waves of snicks as the ball hit bat or pad or boot or pitch – or at any rate came seriously adjacent to them.

Meanwhile, the Jargon Buster was explaining the more obscure terms used by Radio 4's experts, like 'debacle', 'abject surrender' and 'they want their heads chopping off, feeding to rats then sticking on a pikestaff'. The appeal of the game has never been broader.

Sure, there's never going to be any shortage of moaners and groaners bellyaching about England's results and waving record books to show that we are about to go bottom of the coveted *Wisden* World Rankings. You can produce statistics to prove anything. But if there was a disappointment it was the way the lads let the game drift into a meaningless fourth day.

I mean, how many corporate sponsors and their guests are

able to leave the golf course on a Sunday to traipse into London to watch cricket? I would estimate that the crowd that day was composed almost entirely of people who had paid as little as 30 quid to go through the turnstiles. Talk about amateur night.

There's no doubt that our strength as a cricketing nation lies in our networking and corporate outreach skills. You've only got to look at Tuffers in post-match interview mode – pint of Scrumpy Jack in his hand and the rich smoke of a Benson's playing around the mouthpiece of his mobile. The guy's a matchwinner as far as the sponsors are concerned. All credit, then, to the England and Wales Cricket Board. They are doing a tremendous job going out into some of the most ethnic of housing estates in the country, advising youngsters on the kind of skills they need if they want to be professional sportsmen and maybe even become the next Aftab Habib.

There's no shortage of talent out there, it just needs tapping. Dave Podmore's a great believer in Kwik Cricket. This is not, as you might imagine, the fashionable form of five-day cricket which is over inside three, but that game you see kids playing on the outfield in the lunch interval.

The ECB has had the brilliantly proactive idea of adding a marketing element to the game. While the youngsters enjoy a low-alcohol drink they can develop their networking and contact-forging skills. Last Saturday I saw one little lad down in front of the sight screen at the Nursery End. He delivered a text-book after-dinner speech before signing a couple of miniature bats for his pals and saying, 'No problem, great to talk to you.'

Coping with uncalled-for nudity.

Reggae during the lunch interval hasn't worked. Nor has letting the Windies win one or helping Brian Lara get back into form. No question, the Powers That Be have to do much much more to encourage Afro-Caribbean crowds back into the specially designated sections of our Test grounds. For it to continue in a healthy state, this great game (cricket) needs their wonderfully positive outlook on life, and in particular their 36 quids. But how many West Indian streakers have we seen this summer? About the same number as Nass Hussain has scored runs, actually.

It's been suggested that because of a more laid-back lifestyle they tend not to plan their streaking in advance like the English lads do, going on a strict lager and pie-and-chips diet for weeks beforehand so as to be fit for the cameras. Perhaps we could set aside a limited number of Windies streakers' tickets to be sold on the day.

Obviously you'd have to keep the penalties the same or you'd have our friends the race relations do-gooders after you. On the vexed subject of summary punishment for streakers, I don't know if anyone heard the fascinating discussion among the Test Match Special experts during the Old Trafford Test? Pod did, and there's nothing I would have liked more than to join in the free-ranging debate. Sadly I was stuck in the Dartford Tunnel and my Nokia decided that was the moment not to send any e-mails.

But suggestions ranged from putting streakers in a cage and

humiliating them (that came from CM-J, who'd clearly been giving it a lot of thought during the interruptions), to fining them £10,000, confiscating their clothes and sending them home harry starkers on the tram. All appealing in their different ways.

An idea that some of the tabloid boys have come up with would get the Podmore vote. That is, to publish the names and photos of known streakers and encourage county members to take the law into their own hands. The Naming and Shaming and Torching and (Optional) Castrating Initiative might also offer up some alternative ideas as to what to put in those delightful hanging baskets outside the Old Trafford pavilion. If this didn't work then I suppose we'd have to look at closing the bars during the tea interval, but surely that has to be a last resort which can only be bad for the game.

The Academy of Cricketing Excellence: a progress report.

Pod's spent much of the last week under siege from the media, camped outside my picture window with their long telephoto lenses while I lay calmly on my sofa eating a bucket of chocolate chip ice-cream. And showing not a trace of remorse, any more than I did after bowling two consecutive overs of underarm balls to win that Tilcon Trophy match at Nuneaton in 1983.

It seems Dave Podmore is somehow connected with Kate Hoey getting the sack as sports czar. The charge is that giving me £35 million for my Academy of Cricketing Excellence was irresponsible at a time when senior citizens were lying on trolleys in hospital corridors bleating for new hips. My answer is that these people wouldn't need organ replacements had they spent more time in middle age like Dave Podmore, turning their arm over a bit.

Let's just look at what the Academy has achieved so far on just a promise of that big government cheque (it's still in the post according to the guy on the Consignia Help Desk). The Georgian front door's in, the wiring's as safe as it'll ever be and the atrium's there or thereabouts – no mean architectural feat in a Portakabin. So if and when Mister so-called Blair ever decides to get out into the real world and visit a certain trading estate on the outskirts of Leicester he'd see what a pillock he'd made of himself by picking on Hoey-y for the reverse nod treatment.

But it's not just about bricks, mortar and MDF. We're already seeing the fruits of our fledgling enterprise out on the park. It's no exaggeration to say it was one of the greatest moments of Pod's life to see Owais Shah batting at Lord's this week, sharing a record fourth-wicket stand with Banger Trescothick and proudly wearing a big '69' on the back of his shirt. A bit saucy, yes, but just the sort of number that's going to attract the youngsters to the game.

Many other leading international cricketers have already paid their £500 consultation fee to the Academy for choosing that all-important number for their ODI shirts. Our first blue-chip clients were Shane Warne, who opted for 23 after his hero Michael Jordan, and Hansie Cronje (666 after his). Since those guys paved the way demand has been so great that I wouldn't be surprised if we have to put another fax line in.

It's nearly 30 years now since I realised the marketing potential of this idea. I happened to scribble the phone number of a minicab firm in felt-tip on Paul Pridgeon's shirt-tail (Star Cars as I recall – 'U Drink, We Drive'). Pridge has bowled 35 consecutive overs with his back to the local photographer, and Pod's ended up with free rides round Kidderminster for the rest of the season.

As usual I was before my time and it's taken till now for the ECB to come up with their idea of embroidering a guy's Test shirt with a little figure denoting where he comes in the sequence of England players. 'Daddy daddy – Matthew Hoggard's wearing number 7348 – oh please can we go to Edgbaston to try and spot it through a telescope?' You see what I'm getting at – a total yawn, and totally uncommercial.

It's round the other side of the shirt where the real money's to be made. Just this morning I made £500 suggesting Number 6 to fag-meister Phil Tufnell; I banked another monkey after giving Mark Waugh '11–4' and then another, would you believe, for reminding Alec Stewart that '5936/C' was Michael Caine's prisoner-of-war number in his favourite film, *Escape to Victory*. Mark my words, in a few years' time cherished numbers will be changing hands for thousands and Pod will be in Florida, feet up with a pina colada as he leafs through the airmail edition of *East Midlands Autotrader*.

More sensible remedies for anti-social behaviour.

Sometimes you really do despair. For once in his life Dave Pod-more finds himself in agreement with the retired players who fill up our beloved media pages. The continued failure of the Powers That Be to address the crowd problems that have dogged our sport for no fewer than three summer evenings makes you fear for the future of the game. It's got to stop.

Don't get me wrong, there's nothing new in supporters running onto the playing area and if done properly it can add to the atmosphere. For example my own proposal for the lunchtime entertainment during the Saturday of the Lord's Test – a re-enactment by The Sealed Knot of the 1975 World Cup Final crowd invasion – only needs to be rubber-stamped by the MCC's Marvellous Spectacle Committee. If anyone knows where to lay their hands on 4000 pairs of stick-on sideburns they can contact me care of this newspaper.

But there are limits, and this week Pakistan's supporters have overstepped the mark so far that even Shep would have spotted it. Horn-blowing and fireworks are bad enough – at Trent Bridge it was so deafening that there were innocent corporate clients in the hospitality boxes who could barely hear the commentary from Royal Ascot on the TV. True story.

What really gets up Pod's pipe is indiscriminate stump-nicking. These silly youngsters don't seem to realise that they

are literally taking the bread out of the mouths of professional cricketers. With every Tom, Dick and Haroon walking around with a carrier bag full of stumps then obviously it's got to drive down the souvenir auction value. Waqar Younis could have had a truly unforgettable benefit night flogging the Headingley poles as a memento of his seven-for on Sunday. Instead of which he'll be scrabbling around for Goochie's gloves and Hicky's hat and Derek Pringle's pants – all the usual old rubbish.

So those kids who think they are supporting their team by running onto the pitch are actually doing the opposite. Believe me, if this kind of dangerous behaviour is allowed to continue, someone is going to be seriously out of pocket.

And what has our wonderful new government – with its transport minister who can't even drive – done about this descent into total anarchy? Nothing. You just can't legislate for a lack of legislation.

The good news is that now the ICC has announced a more than healthy operating income, the funds exist to tackle the problem. Granted there might not be too much change out of the £9.7 million once they've opened the offices in Monte Carlo. But it should be enough to tool up those hard-working stewards, night-club bouncers and unemployed rugby league players drafted in to enforce a modicum of Yorkshire common sense in those sections of ground where the inflatable aliens are coloured green.

Along with the Test Match Special commentary team I also heartily endorse the idea of a six-foot-deep ditch round the boundary with spikes in the bottom. It's a highly proactive engineering concept and on the Fairmead Trading Estate where the

Dave Podmore Academy of Cricketing Excellence currently pitches its tent there's been talk of little else. Several local contractors have got pound signs for eyeballs including my neighbours at unit 39. It could be just the opportunity the guys at Ditch Solutions have been waiting for.

But why stop there? The South Africans, as so often in the past, are way ahead of the game. They've been using muzzled fighting dogs for years now, patrolling the boundary ropes with trained handlers wearing big things round their arms. With Table Mountain in the background, there's no finer sight to be seen on the cricketing globe.

We need to take a long hard look at the role of dogs in cricket. Derbyshire have made a good start this season by introducing a £10 dog membership policy and I hear Gloucestershire have just gone one better by giving dog members voting rights. All of which can only be good for the game and democracy in general. But what's required is for the ECB to go the extra mile and set up a system of crack dog squads to control the crowds.

As the proud owner of four Rhodesian Ridgebacks and one right rascally Doberman pup, Dave Podmore would be more than happy to contribute his own expertise. Sadly, the days when you could whistle down a pit and up would come a bull terrier fully fit and raring to go are long gone. So Phase One would be to establish a proper training programme with some decent lottery funding. Meanwhile we need to be installing proper dog facilities at all Test grounds and perhaps even looking at the possibility of hospitality dogs to meet and greet. Poodles in French maids' outfits would add a touch of class.

And now the precedent of conceding a match has been set, like we did against Pakistan, Pod can see a time in the not-too-distant future when we lose the toss, concede the Test, unleash the pack on the Western Terrace and sit back to watch five days of proper red-blooded sport – just like in *Gladiator*.

10

The Sexual Politics
Arena

Back-end time is the bit of the cricket season Dave Podmore likes best. For one thing you've got your leaves falling, and around the grounds there's a delightful autumnal absence of punters clogging up the fast food outlets and betting tents, or sitting in the stands offering unwanted opinions about the percentage a guy is giving it on the park.

September is also the wedding month for cricketers. Time to get out the tuxedo and stain remover and form an arch of bats above the happy couple for the local press boys. After all, it's the only chance most of our batsmen get to raise the willow in front of a crowd so there's usually a bumper turn-out at the registry offices.

Air stewardesses with their top caring abilities tend to be the cricketer's wives of choice, so there was a bit of a scare recently about the suggestion that airlines might stop letting passengers on board who they deemed drunk and potentially abusive. Not only would that mean an end to international cricket as we know it, there'd be a catastrophic fall in the global birth-rate if a guy couldn't get to know a stewardess in her cubby-hole and go through with his effort at the end of the season. Had this system been in force at the time I would never have met Jacqui, not to mention Nikki and – perish the thought – I might still be stuck with Nicqui and her fancy ideas about me chewing my food properly.

Don't get me wrong, the current missis and me have had our problems too but that's just made us stronger. Female journalists (lesbians probably) can write what they want about our private life. My dad fought two World Wars in the trenches to vouchsafe Dave Podmore the freedom to be his own man. I've never made a secret of the fact that I'm no monk, although I do quite often dress up as a nun when it's one of the lads' stag nights.

So you won't find anyone better equipped than Pod to discuss the crucial role of wimmos in the battle of the sexes. Or just sex itself, come to that, I'm happy to discuss that too, at any time.

A weekend of domestic bliss.

I'd be the first to hold my hand up and say that Dave Podmore hasn't been the best of fathers. Being away from home so much hasn't made it exactly easy and obviously I've had to go off and play cricket a fair bit as well. So one way and another I've missed some of my kids' most formative years. But all this rain affecting the Championship has meant that I've had the opportunity to remind myself of what children are all about; also where they go to school and what their names are.

What normally happens every other weekend is that Nikki (the First Ex-Wife) drops them off on a Saturday morning at the main gate while Dad's out there on the park sweating cobs to earn the Man of the Match award so I can afford their dinner. Then Sunday evening she'll pick them up on the stroke of six. Never mind if I'm on course for a half-tidy three-for at the end of the AXA, off they go regardless. Under the new Duckworth/Lewis system a lot of games have been finishing early, which has meant that Jacqui (the Bird) and I have been left to look after the kids for up to an hour until their mother arrives, which can lead to a certain amount of emotional wear and tear on a relationship.

So after what happened to the upholstery in her MX5 a fort-night ago, Jacqui stamped her pretty little foot and said, 'You're on your own this weekend, Pod.' Right on cue comes the news that there's going to be no cricket on Saturday and Sunday's a wash-out as well. Fortunately we were playing Derby, who have a deserved reputation for being the most creative wet-weather outfit on the circuit. Sure enough Daffy had heard of a pub just half an hour up the A3053 which not only boasted a big screen but also gave Sainsbury's Reward Points – with double-bubble for Drambuie! And to think this is the man they leave out of the England side.

What's more, and you're not going to believe this, when we arrive in the car park there's only a bouncy castle complete with surveillance camera so you can keep a watchful eye on the kids from the bar and rack up some school vouchers for their education at the same time.

Come midnight, we've all enjoyed what can only be described as the very best in British sport: the Lions taming the Boks, Rusedski-y flying the flag at Wimbledon and, for an encore, the various Derbyshire tendencies settling their differences with a friendly glass-throwing contest in the gents. Only snag was when I went out with a torch to check the kids I found they were starving and wringing wet. To make matters worse, when I got them home Jacqui was still up and spitting blood on account of some bad news earlier in the day from Windsor Castle.

Apparently, the Royal Pageant of the Horse had been rained off, which meant that not only were the Coldstream Guards and their cannons no longer required, nor were Jacqui's services as a hostess. She was to have appeared as a personality nurse (sponsored by Superdrug) in the reconstruction of the ill-fated Charge of the Light Brigade. So the last thing she needs is Pod and his unruly offspring turning up and demanding their tea six hours after the scheduled close of play. 'The Ashes may be coming home, Pod, but you can bugger off back to the little sods' mother,' she said, slamming the spare-room door behind her.

Of course now the kids are wide awake, so I give them a couple of alcopops and stick them in front of the telly. That's when I notice the message light flashing in the corner of the channel changer. It tells me that for a competitive £14.95 there's still time to opt into five hours of quality boxing action from Las Vegas. So I ring the cable boys, give them the nod and next thing we're all sitting down as a family enjoying the pre-match atmosphere. Who says television drives people apart? Not Pod.

What's more, the kids slept right through the Sunday good as gold until Ex-Wife arrives to pick them up at six o'clock. Perfect timing for her to miss seeing her pin-up Tim Henman win!

Momentous times ahead at the MCC.

Dave Podmore yields to no one in his condemnation of sexist practices in the game of cricket. And to be fair no one has shown more commitment than myself to involving the fairer sex in the game at all levels. I've been engaged to at least three hospitality girls for a start, and in Jacqui I have the perfect cricketer's fiancee. No one will defend more strenuously the right of an attractive young woman like Jacqui to attend a day's play wearing a smart outfit and neat make-up. It brightens the place up and gives the Sky boys something to cut away to in between deliveries.

But this is not to say that I'm in favour of them completely taking over the whole game, which on the face of it is what is starting to happen. First there was the woman commentator in the last Test. Don't get me wrong, it's something I'm all in favour of. All I ask is that they should have a sense of humour about their work. Look, if you're on the air with Aggers and Blowers joshing away what's more natural than that you're going to get called 'Knockers'? I've apologised to the lady in question and sent her a bunch of flowers and a couple of spare chocolate mints off my pillow. End of story as far as I'm concerned.

But as I say, Pod's a feminist. It's in the blood. My old mum was a sponsor's girl back in the '50s. She used to walk around the boundary at Ilkeston in a French maid's outfit with a tray of Woodbines. With pin-point accuracy she'd lob packets to the

punters very much as Jumbo the peanut vendor did in Trinidad last week. If only I'd inherited her throwing arm instead of my old man's.

But one thing she never did was moan about being excluded from the corridors of power. I refer of course to the forthcoming vote at Lord's concerning the proposed admission to the MCC of women (or wimmos as we call them in the East Midlands). This has been brewing up for some time. Sir Tim Rice and Ms Germaine Greer put their politically correct heads together after recording an episode of *Call My Bluff* and look what happens. Eighteen thousand poor old sods get woken up from their winter hibernation to be asked, 'Do you want to let the boiler-suited brigade into the Long Room, yes or yes?'

Well, you can't stop history. And if that's the only way for Lord's to qualify for a Lottery wad then so be it. But Pod proposes a few measures to make this bitter pill a little easier to swallow.

Rule 1.1: Every application from a member of the female species to be accompanied by two 10 x 8 photos for approval by the appropriate committee. Bearing in mind of course that even with the 'fast track' admission it'll be 20 years before they get in and most of them are going to be past their best.

Rule 1.2: The girls are going to have to conform to a strict dress code. The wearing of trousers will be permitted but they must be shiny in the seat and made of at least 60% nylon. The legs should be of slightly uneven length and short enough to reveal two inches of sock and/or white ankle, with a straggly bit of thread dangling from one turn-up. A good handful of loose change will be carried in the pocket and jingled during awkward conversational lulls.

Rule 1.3: Shirts will display spots of blood where the collar meets the neck, a consequence of careless shaving.

Rule 1.4: Most importantly, ties must be worn at all times and should contain evidence of a full English breakfast (last-minute Casey Joneses purchased at Paddington permitted).

Rule 1.5: When a lady is offered a drink by another lady in the Members' bar she will reply with the words 'You're a gentleman and a scholar.'

These far-reaching proposals should at least scotch the idea that the average cricketer thinks a woman's place is rolling around on a marble floor like that show-pony Boycs got himself into a bit of trouble with. And they should get me some brownie points when Jacqui and the other lads' wives and fiancees arrive on the big silver bird next week. (If you're reading this, love, don't forget to set the video for *Granada Men and Motors*.)

A helping hand for England's women cricketers.

With Headingley about to decide the outcome of the series against Hansie's boys (unless Hansie's already decided the outcome himself), it's time to turn our attention to the other England cricket team that's been pulling in record crowds, sometimes even reaching double figures – the girls.

Quite frankly they've been letting us down on the park and it's obvious to everybody that what's needed is a wise head on shoulders with a ton of experience to take them in hand. Not literally of course – you have to be very careful what you say these days where wimmos are concerned. Nevertheless Dave Podmore has no hesitation in putting his name forward as the England Women's Team Enforcer.

I think I know my way around the gentler sex. I'm about to embark on my third marriage for starters, and when it comes to the game itself I'm fairly legendary around the circuit for managing to get the tea ladies to give me an extra ham or tongue sandwich. There's no time to lose, what with a three-Test series against Australia starting at Guildford next week. The lasses will be playing for their version of the Ashes, which apparently they made by burning a bat in a wok at Lord's the other day. After lightly drizzling it with linseed oil, I'm told.

This shows the right attitude, though of course the women's game will never quite be the equal of the guys'. That's like saying a Mondeo 2.0i can out-perform the new Probe. Absurd. Don't get me wrong, the Mondeo and I had some great times together, but having just taken delivery of a most acceptable new 2.5i 24V Probe courtesy of Ray Poole (Ford) of Hinckley – nice people, nice prices – I recognise there's no comparison. They just ain't the same animal at all, baby.

But as I say, what the girls can do is take the best elements of our recent trouncing of the Boks, and apply it to their own game. Step One: check the availability of Messrs Mervyn Kitchen and Steve Dunne. Sure, you can spend hours in the nets doing press-ups and watching motivational videos, but in my experience if you're going to be successful at Test level there's no substitute for a string of rank, piss-hole umpiring decisions going your way.

Step Two: wind up the oppo. Notice how Athers was able to get right up Donald's pipe Sunday, out-staring him and generally provoking Mr 89mph into behaving like a big girl's blouse, if you'll pardon the expression. Sledging is also a highly effective strategy and could be the key to seeing off the sheilas, who are full of themselves after white-washing us five-zip in the one-dayers.

Pod suggests a quiet word in the shell-like ears of Karen Rolton or Bronwyn Calver, or even the one who just seems to call herself Magno, along the lines of, 'There's a couple of escaped crocodiles hiding under the covers. Any chance you could round them up and get them back to Chessington?'

And let's not forget Step Three, the most important of all: presentation. Stewie's got the lads wearing their England caps at all times, and I counted no less than 18 lions on Hicky last week-end. Whereas the sloppiness displayed by some of our girls over

189

recent weeks has played no small part in handing the advantage to the Aussies.

I was 110 % behind Paul Allott when he let rip at 'Foxy' Reynard, our quickie, running in with her trousers tucked into her socks. 'Surely she must have some needlework skills,' said Walt, bang on target for once in his life. No way he should have been fined half of his commentary fee for that.

I was against the change from divided skirts to trousers in the first place. I mean, bra-burning's all very well in its place, Pod's all for it actually. But the fact remains that there was no more stirring sight than Rachel Heyhoe-Flint steaming in off a full run, knee-socks, big pair of Mayfields billowing out behind her, giving some old dear from the Colonies one up the snot-box early doors. It brought a big red, white and blue lump to Dave Podmore's throat, I tell you.

So we've got a mountain to climb if we're to regain the form that won us the World Cup in 1993. Regular readers familiar with my views on the importance of team bonding won't be surprised to learn that I've organised an eve-of-Test fancy-dress party in the Hog's Back Moat House. If the England women get as big a buzz from dressing up in men's clothes as the guys do from the frocks, those Ashes won't be leaving the wok this side of the millennium.

A novel approach to on-field strategy.

In the end-of-term reports on their summer tour, the Zimboks came in for some – to Pod's mind – unfair praise regarding a so-called bowling innovation. This entails a guy communicating the type of delivery he's about to bowl to the keeper and the other guys in the slips by using the name of his wife or fiancee.

Dave Podmore's here to tell you that there's nothing new under the sun. When I was at Derby a couple of years back we developed this same tactic, which was known as wimmo-ing. Of course there were some teething troubles to be ironed out, like so many ideas in cricket that are ahead of their time, such as BT's Shane Warne Nuisance Phone Call Screening System.

Wimmo-ing looked okay on paper, though maybe the napkins in the Star of Chesterfield were a bit on the dark red side, making the writing difficult to pick up in a poor light. But there was no reason on earth why it shouldn't have worked perfectly. The bowler called out his current wife/fiancee's name for the slower one. For the quicker one he called out the name of his first wife. If he was trying to keep the batter quiet by sliding one into his pads, then it was the name of the fittest secretary in the membership office. Any of the Benson & Hedges hospitality girls was a low full toss. As for the dipping yorker bowled out of the back of the hand from two yards behind the popping crease, I think you called your dog's name out for that.

All pretty straightforward in other words – but you can't

legislate for a guy having been engaged to at least three Jacquis during a long career serving the game. Dave Podmore would have to put his hand up and claim responsibility for the total meltdown of the system in the first round of the NatWest at Telford. I got so confused I forgot who I was living with at the time, and play had to be held up while I nipped out to the car park to check the other name on my windscreen.

But I still maintain that the principle is sound. After all, if the bowler doesn't know who he's engaged to then the batsman sure as hell won't know either. For those of you who are statistically-minded, the elusive name was Nikki, so I duly held one back and some Shropshire sheep-shagger missed it completely and was very nearly out. No question, wimmo-ing worked but it was thought to be too time-consuming with guys having to consult bits of paper before every ball, and it soon went the way of Dennis Lillee's aluminium bat.

Like fractures, multiple fiancees are part and parcel of the modern game – the danger being that sometimes a guy can't even have a benefit match organised in his honour without the ex's sprogs turning up and claiming part of the loot. This is one of the drawbacks of being a high-profile celebrity athlete. During one of Pod's own recent benefits, I suddenly became aware that not all the people gathering round the boundary were well-wishers.

I was so distracted by the sight of some of these alleged mothers letting their kids help themselves to the money in the blankets that I got myself run out, and was met on my return to the pavilion by several gentlemen from the Child Support Agency. Fortunately a few of them were keen cricketers, and to cut a long story short I organised a 25-over thrash and hog roast between a Dave Podmore Dependants' XI and a CSA XI, and we split the takings and called it quits.

Errors in Prime Minister's speech to the WI repeated.

I hear that in pubs and clubs throughout the land they're still talking about Pod's appearance in front of the Beeston branch of the Women's Institute. Well, let them. It was an honest mistake which anybody could have made, and in actual fact it was made by my now ex-manager.

Everyone on the circuit will tell you that no way hasn't Dave Podmore got a lot of time for our friends, the ladies. Call me old-fashioned but I still think it's important when starting the car to lean across a member of the fairer sex and fasten her seat belt first. The half-dozen or so fiancees in my life would willingly stand up in court and give evidence of that. They may have to.

When I got the call telling me that the WI were in the market for one of my celebrated after-dinner speeches, I naturally thought it meant the West Indies boys. And on being confronted by a sea of pleated skirts, I even more naturally thought that Roger Harper had initiated a pre-Test bonding session by getting all the guys into fancy dress. That's one area of their game where the Windies have always been weak (and I know Duncan Fletcher is determined to make Team England's traditional cross-dressing superiority count in the coming months).

From my times in the Caribbean I know that your average calypso cricketer likes his humour the way he likes his swordfish and ackees – salty. I tailored my speech accordingly. But no, they weren't cricketers in those frocks. They were wimmos. What's more, they were in no mood for anything that smacked of politics.

Normally I steer well clear of that kind of material in my 'Twenty Minutes Of No-Holds-Barred Gents' Entertainment'. But if you're taking a sideways look at people's ethnic differences, or making one or two tongue-in-cheek suggestions about sterilising unmarried mothers – well, it's fairly predictable that the goats of certain WI harridans are going to be got up.

At first I took no notice of the booing and slow handclaps – after all, I've had to put up with that right through my career. But when some old biddy at the back (whom I thought was Courtney Walsh) started calling out, 'What about childcare, Pod?' I suspected something wasn't right. The upshot is that I'm facing criminal prosecution under various sections of various Acts of Parliament, not to mention staring down both barrels of an ICC life ban.

The last word - from Dave Podmore's better half.

When the editor discovered that David wouldn't be available to write his column this week on account of doing 200 hours' community service, he asked if I (or 'the lovely and mysterious Jacqui' as he kindly put it!) would be interested in sitting in. My first thought was: Yikes!!! I hadn't been that nervous since the time I had to carry a tray of pints past the Western Terrace dressed as a French maid – me that is, the Barmy Army had all come as nuns.

But then my second thought was: why not?! After all, David and I are partners . . . he's always saying things like 'You know what Jac', you and Pod go together like Athers and Banger, or B & Q.' So it was a case of come on Jacqui, pull yourself together, show them you're more than just a Benson & Hedges trophy wife. Now's your chance to answer the question everyone's been asking since the court case started: How can you stand by this man? A man whose boobs are bigger than yours? And how do you manage to do it always looking 150% perfectly groomed and never losing that bubbly personality?

Well, to answer the last point first, Jacqui Podmore is a professional. I've represented more blue-chip corporate sponsors than Dave Podmore has represented countries or counties or whatever they call them. And to answer the first question, simple. My David is innocent. He says there is no evidence whatsoever that those 54 Sunshine coaches never reached the Kurdish kiddies and I believe him. That man did eight bungee jumps in two weeks, several in the nude, to help raise the money. He even did one with Caprice and he deserves a sodding medal for that.

Now he wouldn't have gone to all that trouble if he was simply going to put all the money in our Bradford and Bingley 'Top Brass' account, would he? Anyway David has no head for figures – apart from mine! – and he's so modest he never talks about his bowling average, which I happen to know is more than 100. Though I was a bit surprised when the diary appeared in court saying he'd been in all sorts of places I knew he hadn't.

But as I said to the judge, who took a bit of a shine to me actually, I'm not a person who attaches much importance to Fidelity. She's just a stripper basically, making out she's a cabaret artiste, and her real name's not Fidelity anyway. It's Joyce Wilkinson and my mum was at school with her.

Whatever the rights and wrongs of the situation, the upshot is that I've got to work my derriere off (pardon my French) to earn the money while his nibs is off dredging canals. Which means this weekend for example I've got to be at both of the Cheltenham and Gloucester semi-finals: today it's Taunton in the Scrumpy Jack tent (bikini with apples on etc.). Couple of hours' sleep with the chair against the door then I've got to get into the MX5, drive up to Leicester and get that sexy giggle going all over again, remembering that the boys from Peterborough Pallet Solutions will be hearing it for the very first time.

It's a living on the cricket sash-and-stiletto circuit and a damn good one if you're prepared to work. But like David, Jacqui Podmore hasn't always had the rub of the green careerwise. When he was making his way at Leicester I was a Princess Diana lookalike, then it all went pear-shaped, and while he went to Derby I moved on to Jill Dando – only for us both to run into the same brick wall of unfairness again.

Some of us attract bad luck whereas others only have to spend five seconds in a broom cupboard with Boris Becker and they're set up for life. But Jacqui Podmore is one tough lady. A few Kahluas and a Bridget Jones vid and she bounces back fizzier and dizzier than ever.

So I'm still hopeful of getting the nod, as my fella calls it, to help the boys salvage some self-respect against the Aussies. I was once talked about in the tabloids as being the next Ian Botham's alleged bit on the side. And the next Derek Pringle's, and the next Chris Lewis's. The only reason the phone stopped ringing was because I had to change my mobile number after the business last year with Shane Warne.

Surely the Powers That Be must soon realise the potential of a honey-trap strategy, and when the call comes I won't let anyone down. Fair play to the British Airways stewardesses, they played a blinder trying to keep the Aussies strapped in their seats so they'd pick up deep vein thrombosis niggles. You can't not take your headscarf off to that kind of team effort but it didn't come off on the day, so it's time for fresh faces.

As far as I'm concerned the series is very far from over. There are hotels in Leeds, aren't there? With broom cupboards? It's all about pride now.

Pod's Footnote

Miaaaow!